anxious

choosing faith in
a world of worry

amy simpson

IVP Books
An imprint of InterVarsity Press
Downers Grove, Illinois

InterVarsity Press
P.O. Box 1400, Downers Grove, IL 60515-1426
World Wide Web: www.ivpress.com
Email: email@ivpress.com

InterVarsity Press® is the book-publishing division of InterVarsity Christian Fellowship/USA®, a movement of students and faculty active on campus at hundreds of universities, colleges and schools of nursing in the United States of America, and a member movement of the International Fellowship of Evangelical Students. For information about local and regional activities, write Public Relations Dept., InterVarsity Christian Fellowship/USA, 6400 Schroeder Rd., P.O. Box 7895, Madison, WI 53707-7895, or visit the IVCF website at www.intervarsity.org.

While all stories in this book are true, some names and identifying information in this book have been changed to protect the privacy of the individuals involved.

Cover design: Cindy Kiple
Interior design: Beth McGill
Images: Michael Duva/Getty Images

ISBN 978-0-8308-4314-5 (print)
ISBN 978-0-8308-9653-0 (digital)

Printed in the United States of America ∞

Library of Congress Cataloging-in-Publication Data

Simpson, Amy.
    Anxious : choosing faith in a world of worry / Amy Simpson.
        pages cm
    Includes bibliographical references.
    ISBN 978-0-8308-4314-5 (pbk. : alk. paper)
    1. Worry—Religious aspects—Christianity. 2. Anxiety—Religious
aspects—Christianity. 3. Trust in God—Christianity. I. Title.
    BV4908.5.S53 2014
    248.8'6—dc23
                                                                    2014022808

P 22 21 20 19 18 17 16 15 14 13 12 11 10 9 8 7 6 5 4 3 2 1

Y 32 31 30 29 28 27 26 25 24 23 22 21 20 19 18 17 16 15 14

This book is dedicated to Trevor,

who walks with me through worry

and reminds me to believe what's true;

To my sisters, Cheryl and Kate,

who have shared so many of my worries

and traveled with me toward greater trust in

the One who has always been there for us;

And to my children,

my greatest reasons for worry;

With all thanks and gratitude to God,

who loves me despite my worry

and is my only reason not to.

Contents

Introduction

Let me start by telling you what this book is not.

This is not a book with five easy steps to free yourself from anxiety. It offers some practical advice, but ultimately it is focused less on changing behavior and more on letting God transform the way we see him—and ourselves by comparison.

This book is not a substitute for counseling or therapeutic understanding. It does attempt to define and clarify differences between fear, anxiety and worry, and as you read, I hope it will lead to a better understanding of yourself. But its soul is theological and spiritual, not psychological or medical.

This book is not written to shame people who have anxiety disorders and who often hide in fear that others will judge them for their lack of control over anxious thoughts and feelings and the physical symptoms that threaten to overwhelm them. Historically, our society is quick to judge such disorders, to chalk them up to personal weakness or sin or demonic control, to prescribe more faith or more prayer or just getting over it. But anxiety disorders are illnesses with very real physical and emotional symptoms, and there's no more shame in this than any other kind of illness. The remedy is not in a book; it's in medical help and sound counseling to help retrain runaway thoughts and beliefs that fuel emotions.

This is a book primarily for the rest of us, who think worry is a problem for "those worriers." Ironically, while we're so quick to judge people who can't control their anxiety, we go very easy on ourselves if we can control our anxiety—even if we choose not to. Many of us believe a certain amount of worry is perfectly OK, even commendable. As long as we stay in control, as long as our worry doesn't become "excessive," it's not a problem.

And yet it is a problem. It's our very control that indicts us. While some may not choose to worry, the rest of us actually do. Such a choice is an act of rebellion against God, who requires our trust. And we're far more worried than we think we are.

This is a book for people like me, who, until the last few years, never thought I was a worrier. I was so accustomed to living with a certain level of fear that I felt but couldn't see, I truly believed I didn't have a problem with worry. And yet each day I moved from worry to worry, fueled by an anxiety so constant I noticed it only when it spiked to a level higher than usual. I allowed it to alter my course, mute my sense of calling, keep me quiet when I should have spoken and keep me speaking when I should have been silent.

That is, until God's Holy Spirit confronted me with the way God describes himself in his Word. He pointed out descriptions of his power, sovereignty, infinite nature and goodness, and these biblical passages painted vivid pictures for me—pictures I hadn't really seen before. I began to see how weak and tenuous my trust was by comparison. And I began to notice a theme throughout God's story, a call for people to release their cradling hold on fear, turn away from it and trust him. This theme goes far beyond the "don't worry" passages so frequently quoted on refrigerator magnets and weaves its way through familiar stories I now saw through a new lens.

Worry is not the same as fear; it's the practice of indulging fear, clinging to it, feeding and serving it. Worry is a cheap substitute for productive action and for surrender to someone with capabilities and perspective far beyond our own. For many of us, our relationship with worry is even more perverse: we wave it as a flag of self-importance, fly it over our own castles and kingdoms to proclaim to the world around us that we are responsible, capable, indispensable.

This is not an uncommon condition. Erecting our own castles, in monument to ourselves and in defense of all we think we possess, is a distinctly human activity. And we live in a culture that expects such worried kingdom building. Anyone without a castle is out in the cold. And anyone without a flag of worry is likely to be overlooked or disdained as irresponsible, uninterested, unaware.

But just because such a practice is definitively human doesn't mean it's harmless. Anyone familiar with the effects of anxiety and fear knows they can destroy a person. And this destruction is not limited to our physical selves; a lifestyle of worry is incompatible with a life of faith. A castle of our own, erected by our own pride, forms a wall between us and God, and must be dismantled lovingly by a generous King who invites us into his kingdom, a kingdom that needs no wall, a fortress of impenetrable strength, a place of welcome and love and beauty and peace that will never be abandoned.

In this age, as in all ages, we are most sensitive to the sins that violate prevailing cultural norms in addition to God's standards: in our current climate, sins like theft, infidelity, murder, cruelty, abuse. But we struggle even to see the ones that are camouflaged in our society: consumerism, self-absorption, self-righteousness, selfish ambition. And worry. It's in the water we drink and use for washing.

This book will help you see the poison in the water and the pervasive presence of worry in your own life. It's a book designed to confront and transform the culture among people who follow Jesus. To challenge us all to be set apart by our refusal to buy into the illusions of control and possession and to engage in the practice of worry so prevalent in the world around us. We must let go of the mistaken belief that life can and should be safe. That our powers extend farther than what God has granted us. That our chief purpose in this life is to avoid danger and accumulate treasures. That we possess and must preserve that which actually belongs to God. That the future, where all our greatest hopes and worries lie, is a promise we can claim for ourselves.

For human pride, a look at God's Word is full of bad news. It simply does not affirm what we want so badly to believe about ourselves. But for those humble enough to acknowledge that the one who created the very boundaries that define our understanding of the universe has knowledge and power we can't understand, there is very good news. That powerful one is good and loving and unthinkably generous with us. He welcomes us into his very family, asking only that we live by faith. In him is every reason to live a countercultural life, a life that is not defined by worry.

Anxious will encourage you to live that kind of countercultural, counterintuitive life in response to who God is. It will challenge you to see your own worried habits and to remember the words of Jesus: "Can all your worries add a single moment to your life?" (Mt 6:27). Ultimately, it will nudge you toward the God who offers spiritual freedom and rest to all whose hearts are troubled.

1

frantic

Should you be worried?

Well, if you're like me, and in this regard I feel confident that you are, you have many reasons to worry. And you probably spend a lot of time and energy worrying—but you haven't admitted it yet. This book is written for people like you: people who aren't convinced worry is a problem in their lives. People who don't even know they're imprisoned and so can't envision freedom. So let me start by saying you are worried. And now I'll tell you why.

As I write this, I'm keeping one eye on my backyard, where a small lake has formed after two days of relentless and sometimes violent storms. I'm praying for the rain to stop and the waters to recede. I'm thinking about my friends and neighbors who have basements full of water and boats floating down their suburban streets, and I'm worrying that my house will flood as well. Ironically, just a few months ago, I was worried about a drought that threatened not only the local area but most of the nation's agriculture.

A quick glance at the news will remind me of a thousand other, bigger reasons to worry. Terrorism can and does strike anywhere, at any time. We face a growing global nuclear threat. Climate change, which might have something to do with the droughts and floods

literally in my own backyard, is making our natural world less pre-
dictable—and we don't know where it will lead us. Unemployment
and economic recession threaten the well-being of so many families.
Public rhetoric is brash and angry. Religions and worldviews clash
bitterly. Diseases spread globally. Animals face extinction while non-
native species thrive in places they never should be living.

The news is bleeding with stories of mass murder, gun violence,
genocide, war, rape, suicide and other forms of violence. The World
Health Organization tells us fifteen thousand people die each day
from injuries of all kinds. That's one person every five seconds.[1] In
many parts of the world, gender-based discrimination wages war
against women and girls. And my own preteen and teenage girls, like
all American kids their age, stand at the edge of a world brimming
with more choices than they can possibly make on their own, a world
that places very few limits on what they can do but would happily
consume them—that is staged to lure them into self-destruction, ad-
diction and lies that promise greater freedom among the yawning,
gleaming, pretty teeth of cruel traps.

And if you can't see enough reasons to worry, consider what you
can't see.

Consider the microscopic world of bacteria and antibiotics. In this
age of relatively easy access to health care (compared with generations
before), our liberal use of antibiotics is working against us. When we
treat disease with antibiotics, a few bacteria sometimes survive the
treatment. For example, the antibiotic or the dosage may not be strong
enough to wipe out the entire infection. Sometimes a single bacteria
organism manages to repel the treatment. And often patients fail to
finish all their prescribed medication once they feel better. In such cases,
the bacteria learn how to fight and survive antibiotic attack, and they
develop resistance to those antibiotics. They become harder (or even
impossible) to contain and kill with the weapons we have. Those strong
bacteria multiply and create difficult and expensive treatment challenges.

This is not only a human problem. Antibiotics are regularly used to treat animals raised for food, to promote growth and to prevent infection in healthy animals. As a result of this practice, which some livestock growers are now abandoning, animal-borne bacteria develop resistance to antibiotics and our food supply is contaminated with harmless but strong bacteria we don't have effective weapons to fight. When we eat such food, this strong bacteria takes up residence in our bodies and builds up over time. When we get infections, the strong genes from that bacteria may render the harmful bacteria in our bodies resistant to treatment.

Development of antibiotics (following Alexander Fleming's discovery of penicillin in 1928) dramatically altered the course of human history. Millions of lives have been saved through the use of such drugs, and diseases that once terrorized our ancestors (such as scarlet fever and pneumonia) now constitute moderate inconveniences for most people with access to good medical care and early intervention, requiring only a quick visit to the doctor, ten days of treatment and a few days in bed. Antibiotics are awesome when they kill bacteria. But as with humans, that which doesn't kill bacteria makes it stronger—and that's when antibiotics hurt us. So every time someone uses antibiotics unnecessarily or fails to finish the entire course of medication, that person is contributing to a larger health crisis that potentially could render our most potent weapon against disease ineffective.[2]

The problem doesn't stop there. In our efforts to be clean, we may be encouraging disease. Antibacterial hand soap and household cleaners, like low doses of antibiotics, actually encourage the growth of strains of bacteria that not only resist cleaning but may cause antibiotic-resistant diseases. Along with the bad, antibacterial hand soap can remove good bacteria from our hands—bacteria that help us fight disease. Cleaners of all kinds teach bacteria how to fight back and stay alive on surfaces we then use for cooking and eating. And when these soaps and cleaners are washed into the water supply and that water is used for agriculture, they increase the risk that our food supply is contaminated with more bacteria that have learned how to survive our efforts to kill them. Ironically, scientists say there is no real benefit to using products like antibacterial hand soap in most homes. They don't keep us healthier or cleaner than regular soap, which does a good job of removing bacteria so we actually don't need to try to kill them. Yet many homes are routinely stocked with antibacterial products.[3]

Basically, the harder we try to be clean and healthy, the more we risk a bacteria-based global health crisis, the very thing we're trying to avoid.

So do we have reason to worry? You bet we do—about all this and more. And our culture tells us worrying is not only justified; it's the right thing to do. If you aren't worried, you are either (1) dead, (2) comatose or (3) seriously out of step with our culture.

But while our culture tells us one thing, God tells us another. He tells us not to worry. And yes, he is fully aware of all the reasons we think we should worry. He tells us to expend our energy instead on exercising faith in him and his character. Embracing faith is the one human choice God values most—above showing kindness, trying to be good and following all the rules. One cannot love God—the greatest commandment—without exercising faith. Faith is what turns our ordinary acts of love into acts in service to God. Faith is the one thing without which he tells us "it is impossible to please God" (Heb 11:6).

Unless you're a tremendously unique person, you worry. And because of the environment we live in, you may not even recognize it. Worry is a rebellious choice we usually don't take very seriously. But it is serious. Willful worry amounts to rejection of God's character and damages our capacity for the life he calls us to. A close look at Scripture shows us worry has always been a frequent point of correction between God and his people because it undermines that very faith he requires and rewards. Worry is still chronically undermining the faith and courage of Christians in this age. It is rooted in a theological misunderstanding of who God is, the nature of life in this world and our place in the universe. Overcoming worry starts not with a list of therapeutic steps but with a reorientation around the truth about God, who is not threatened by what scares us.

FEAR: AN ILLUSTRATION

Speaking of what scares us, let's consider a definition of worry and what makes it different from fear and anxiety. The three concepts—fear, worry and anxiety—are often confused and mentioned interchangeably, but they are different and should be thought of differently. In addressing the problem of worry, it's critical that we separate it from the normal, healthy and productive capabilities God gave us in fear and, to some degree, anxiety. It's also important to differentiate worry from anxiety disorders, which require a different understanding and approach.

When I think of these differences, I am reminded of an experience I had several years ago. I was working as a freelance writer in the basement of a house my husband and I rented in Alaska. We were expecting our first child and training a growing puppy. While my husband was at work, I was working on a writing project when the dog started whining. It took a while for her whining to break my concentration, and even then I decided to ignore it for a few more minutes. But when the barking started, I knew I had to pay attention.

I turned away from my computer screen and toward the eyes of our adorable and amusing young golden retriever, Molly. She was staring at me with urgency, the same kind of look Lassie used to communicate that someone had fallen into a well.

I sighed and looked out the window at the distressed and sputtering sunlight of an Alaskan winter afternoon and accepted that it was time for a break—for both me and Molly. A high-energy puppy without a fenced yard, Molly needed frequent short walks. And at eight months pregnant, so did I.

I stretched my back, squeezed into my winter coat and waddled over to get the leash, while Molly paced in the general vicinity of the door, whining and snuffling and growing more agitated. "Hang on, Molly. I'm moving as fast as I can," I said with a bit of impatience.

When I had hooked the leash to her collar, I opened the door and shrugged against a swipe of subzero air. "Let's get this over with." But when I tugged at the leash, Molly balked and refused to go outside. "You've got to be kidding," I groaned. It was cold, but not too cold for a quick trip to the side yard to take care of business. And now that I was bundled up, I was determined to make it happen. So I pulled harder on the leash, thankful that she was still small enough that even in my clumsy condition I could get her to move across the snow's slick frozen crust.

As I carefully made my way over the treacherous, bumpy surface, Molly stopped a couple of times, momentarily refusing to go any farther. Each time, I pulled on the leash and made her keep going, wondering why she was suddenly so wimpy about the cold. I had never known her to pass up an opportunity for some much-needed relief and a minute to exercise her wonderfully sensitive nose in the outside air.

When we approached the corner of the house, she finally sat down in the snow and pulled back on the leash so firmly I lost my footing and nearly fell. She started barking again, right at me, again reminding me of Lassie.

As I struggled to regain my balance, my irritation with the dog suddenly turned to gasping fear as I caught site of a huge, dark shape in my peripheral vision. I turned my head and looked straight at the hulking chest of an adult moose—standing just around the corner of the house, staring down at me from four feet away.

Suddenly I realized Molly and I had had a terrible misunderstanding.

I was pretty impressed with how fast I moved back across that icy, rugged snow.

Back in the house, I apologized to Molly and she agreed to "hold it" for a while. So we settled in for the rest of the afternoon and watched the moose and her calf graze on the trees in our yard. I vowed to listen to my dog next time she barked and then suggested it might be best to stay inside for a while.

That's fear.

My fear was sensible, powerful and potentially life-saving. My dog's fear was too. If you haven't seen a moose in the wild, you should know it's an awe-inspiring sight. They're huge animals. And while generally peaceable, if they feel the need to defend themselves or their calves (from a barking dog named Molly, for example), they can be deadly. They're also surprisingly fast: one thousand pounds of muscle running at speeds up to thirty-five miles per hour. A slow, pregnant lady waddling across the ice-crusted snow would stand no chance.

When I saw that moose up close, I didn't hesitate. I didn't have to decide what to do—my fear did the work for me, causing my body to respond by running away—much faster than I thought I could. This is one way fear helps us—it can literally keep us alive.

Fear Versus Anxiety

Merriam-Webster's dictionary defines fear as "an unpleasant often strong emotion caused by anticipation or awareness of danger." When a person feels fear, a surge of hormones—most notably adrenaline—triggers a response in the body: the heart and lungs work faster, muscles tense, the skin flushes or grows pale, the pupils dilate, and the senses may become either dulled or hyper-alert. While some people embrace the "rush" of fear in a controlled environment, no one would want to live in this emotional state all the time. But as unpleasant as it might be, fear is a gift. When we feel fear in response to danger, it motivates us to protect ourselves and others by hiding, running away or fighting. Danger arrives in many forms—physically, emotionally, psycho-logically—and fear should be our immediate response to all of them. If we lived in a perfect world, we would have no need for fear. But in the world we inhabit, the fear response is not only necessary—it's healthy.

There is a subtle difference between fear and anxiety, and it's not in the emotions themselves—it's in what they're responding to. Merriam-Webster's defines anxiety as "painful or apprehensive uneasiness of mind usually over an impending or anticipated ill." Anxiety usually appears not in the face of an immediate threat, as with fear, but when anticipating something that will or might happen.

Kaplan and Sadock's Concise Textbook of Clinical Psychiatry explains it this way:

> Anxiety is an alerting signal; it warns of an impending danger and enables a person to take measures to deal with a threat. Fear is a similar alerting signal, but it should be differentiated from anxiety. Fear is a response to a known, external, definite, or non-conflictual threat; anxiety is a response to a threat that is unknown, internal, vague, or conflictual.[4]

Like fear, anxiety can be a normal, healthy response to stress. It can produce a similar physical effect as fear, and at the right level this physical response (the surge of chemicals like adrenaline, heightened sensory awareness, quick reflexes) can help us perform well when facing a challenge. For example, after my close encounter with Mother Moose, I was more vigilant about going outside, especially in the winter when many moose came down from the mountains in search of food. When I went out my front door, a mild sense of anxiety reminded me to pay attention to signs that a moose might be nearby. This was smart, practical and reasonable.

Here's another helpful example, also from *Kaplan and Sadock's Concise Textbook of Clinical Psychiatry:*

> The emotion caused by a rapidly approaching car as a person crosses the street differs from the vague discomfort a person may

experience when meeting new persons in a strange setting. The main psychological difference between the two emotional responses is the suddenness of fear and the insidiousness of anxiety.[5]

In general, fear is a response to an immediate and known threat. Anxiety is a response to a possibility.

Although both fear and anxiety may help us in the short term, neither is a healthy place to stay. They should motivate us to appropriate and effective action, then go away as soon as they're not needed. Unfortunately, some of us choose to stay in this place of unease by indulging in worry. And for others, staying in a state of anxiety is not a choice.

After the body's initial involuntary fear response, we reach a point where our voluntary system can take over. This might happen a split second after the initial fear—when you realize the spider that landed on your shoulder is, in fact, made of plastic and hanging from your friend's finger—or after a much longer period, having found some measure of safety from the initial danger. This stage may be accompanied by a low dose of productive anxiety—the kind that motivates us to seek answers to our problems and to produce solutions that prevent future danger. At this point, we get to decide how we're going to respond to the world around us, including the danger we just perceived. We should be able to settle ourselves, assess the situation, and either move on in safety or make a plan for handling the ongoing threat in a more deliberate manner.

For some people, things start to go wrong at this point, when their bodies and minds refuse to "shut off" the fear response. Adrenaline and other chemicals continue to course through them and keep their hearts racing. Their bodies, believing a threat is imminent, remain convinced that they must flee or fight an imaginary enemy. Anxiety disorders and panic attacks keep people captive to fear, feeling sick and unable to think clearly until the episode passes or medication and therapy intervene.

For example, after I saw the moose up close, an anxiety disorder could have kept me from venturing outside my house, literally held captive by the possibility that a moose would reappear and trample me. Or a panic attack could have kept my body stuck in that fear response, hormones racing through my system, leaving me unable to function even though I knew my chances of a deadly moose encounter were slim. Such attacks can occur without warning and without any specific reason for fear—even if I had never seen a moose. For other people who experience serious trauma, the fear response will continue to haunt them in the form of post-traumatic stress disorder, a severe anxiety disorder. This disorder is debilitating and generally requires professional help to find healing. (For more on this, see appendix A in this book, "A Word About Anxiety Disorders.")

ENTER WORRY

For most people, once the initial fear and anxious responses have surged and begun to ebb, the voluntary system does take over as it was designed to do. But rather than let go of fear, we sometimes decide to cling to it and embrace it, pouring our energy into keeping it alive. We add each new fear to the large pile of internal fuel waiting to feed the habitual worry that's slowly burning a hole in our soul.

Merriam-Webster defines worry as "mental distress or agitation resulting from concern usually for something impending or anticipated." Unlike fear, worry is not an immediate response to real or perceived danger; it's anticipatory, rooted in concern about something that may or may not happen. Unlike normal anxiety, it's not an involuntary physical response but a pattern we choose to indulge. It rises not from outside us but from within. Whether we realize it or not, worry is an action. It's a choice we make to stay in that place of anxiety that was designed to protect us from immediate danger, not to see us through everyday life.

According to renowned psychiatrist Dr. Edward Hallowell, "Worry is a special form of fear. It is what humans do with simple fear once it reaches the part of their brain called the cerebral cortex. We make fear complex, adding anticipation, memory, imagination, and emotion."[6] Worry is not a helpful activity that moves us forward; it's a repetitive cycle that keeps us stuck. Like a dog "worrying a bone," we protectively guard our fears, focus on them, bury them and dig them back up, examine them, shake them, rearrange them, and gnaw at them even though they can't sustain us.

A PROCESS FOR CHANGE

There is hope; we don't have to be slaves to worry. This book will lead you through a process of not only understanding worry and recognizing its destructive presence in your own life but also embracing an "alternative lifestyle": a way of living that includes healthy fear and accepts the anxiety response that helps protect us, but that rejects the habit of worry and replaces it with a habit of looking to God in trust and seeing life through a perspective informed by his.

This process may require—and produce—change in you. It starts with seeing and admitting to worry in your life. Most people don't like to admit to problems with worry. "Worrywarts" are the ones with worry problems. They're unattractive people who worry too much and create stress for the people around them. As long as you can imagine or identify people who worry more than you do, you might figure you're doing all right.

But just because other people might be more anxious than you are doesn't mean your worry doesn't matter. Until you're aware of how worry affects you, you won't be ready to reject it and begin to change. Take some time to actually think about what makes you worry, how you express your worry and how destructive it is for your faith, your health, your relationships. Acknowledge this to God. And as you work your way through this book, you might come to a greater understanding of your own worry problem.

The next step is to repent of worry. Yes, I know *repent* is an unpopular word with a bad reputation. But it's also a biblical word that describes exactly what we need to do with our acts of rebellion against God. Repentance is an act of contrition and rejection, completely stopping your established momentum and turning around to go in the opposite direction. In prayer, confess your sinful obsession with seeking to live in God's domain, to be like God in ways you weren't created to be, and choose to reject worry from now on. That most likely doesn't mean you'll never worry again, but it affirms your serious desire to stop and your commitment to fight your inclination. It serves to open the door to God's work.

I encourage you to go through this process of recognition and repentance now or as you work your way through this book and consider the destructive presence of worry in your own life.

Finally, seek medical or psychological help if you need it—if you can't stop worrying, you experience physical effects from anxiety (especially if they come out of the blue) or anxiety is interfering with your ability to function as you normally have. Seeking help is not a cop-out or a sign of weakness. It is a way to help you manage symptoms of anxiety so that you can work on the real issues and pursue the trusting, peace-filled and courageous kind of life God wants you to live. If you need more information about this, you may find some helpful insights in appendix A at the back of this book.

Fear and anxiety can be healthy and productive. They can trigger an automatic, lifesaving response. They can motivate us to make wise choices, rescue others and manage risk. Worry, on the other hand, is destructive, unproductive and wasteful. Yet most of us engage in it regularly, perhaps in more ways than we realize.

2

Our Worried World

Many of us—and the society we live in—are frantic with worry. Worry is part of our culture, an expectation of responsible people. We seem to equate worry with good citizenship and awareness. We are expected to remain on emotional "high alert" as evidence that we care about the world around us. Our attitude is, to paraphrase a bit of bumper-sticker wisdom, "If you're not worried, you're not paying attention."

Most of us don't even realize we're consumed with worry. When I asked several people to tell me about their experiences with worry, most indicated they don't consider themselves "worriers." Then they went on to tell me about their struggles with worry, some of them describing sleepless nights and disruptions to relationships caused by worry. A few described panic attacks and other symptoms of runaway anxiety. But almost no one wanted to be labeled a "worrier."

A friend of mine wrote an article about her experience when she tried fasting from worry during Lent. This laid-back woman had never considered herself a worrier, and yet God used this experience to reveal a powerful dependence on worry. She realized she often worried that she would be attacked when she was alone. Her husband went out of town for two weeks, and she had to resist the urge to keep checking and rechecking the locks as she usually did. Then she found herself lost in a city overseas and fighting panic. Through it all, she learned that she was prone to carry responsibilities God had not given her. She also learned to let go of her usual worried reactions and trust God for protection and guidance.[1]

I never thought I was a worrier either, until God lovingly started showing me the pervasive presence of worry in my life and giving me momentary glimpses of freedom from worry. I will now readily admit that I am a worrier, desperately pursuing freedom through trust in God—based in a stronger, deeper theology of who God is and who I am called to be. In fact, as I write this book, I'm tremendously worried that I don't have enough to say, that no one will buy this book and help feed my family, that I'm the only person who doesn't have control over the problem of worry—and here I am stupidly admitting it to everyone. I need this book as much as anyone.

Our reasons for worrying so much are embedded in the world around us. And we are surrounded not only by reasons to worry but also by people who want us to worry because it makes them feel better about themselves or because there is profit in fueling our fear. Whether we realize it or not, we are under pressure to conform to a self-feeding culture of worry.

MANUFACTURED WORRY

In his 1999 book *The Culture of Fear,* Barry Glassner describes how powerful people play on our fears for the sake of getting our attention, enriching themselves or making themselves even more powerful. He addresses several societal scares that were exaggerated or even invented, but which haunted the national conscience: things like road rage, violent crime waves, health risks and travel safety. In the book's introduction he says, "The short answer to why Americans harbor so many misbegotten fears is that immense power and money await those who tap into our moral insecurities and supply us with symbolic substitutes."[2]

Glassner argues that focusing on these problems, blown out of proportion or even trumped-up, distracts us from paying attention to what actually matters and what we might be able to change. This culture of fear plays on our anxieties, coming and going without resolution, moving from one fear to the next, leaving a residual sense that we must do something—so we worry over things that may or may not be significant or even real.

Then again, some of what worries us is all too real.

Work Worries

Good employees worry about their jobs. We really worry when the economy is not booming—but we don't stop when things are going well. We worry about losing our jobs, finding jobs, getting noticed at work, being asked to do more than we can handle, not being challenged, making the right impression, being overlooked for advancement, not getting everything done, making mistakes and keeping our organizations afloat. Some of us work too many hours, long past the point of productivity, simply because we can't bring ourselves to let go and walk away. Others stop working at the end of the day but mentally never leave work. While they're technically engaged with their families, friends and God, they are always giving the best part of their thought life to worrying about work.

When I worked as a publishing executive, I had a hard time mentally leaving my work at the office and fully engaging with my family when I was home. On occasion, I would actually get irritated with my husband and children for interrupting my thoughts about work with requests, stories about their days and calls to "Watch this, Mom!" On those days, my physical presence wasn't worth much to my family because I wasn't engaged mentally and emotionally. And worse, I sacrificed my time with them for what? Not even productive work—I was simply worrying over the day that had been and the days to come, none of which were true realities in the present. I missed out on some important moments with the people I say matter most in my life—not because I wasn't there, but because my mind wasn't present.

PARENTING

Speaking of families, good parents worry about their kids, right? That's how we show we care. We worry that they're not eating right, that they're eating too much or too little, that they don't have enough friends, that they have too many of the wrong friends, that they don't have the right clothes or the right attitude. We worry that their grades aren't high enough, that their backpacks are too heavy, that they aren't having enough fun in school, that they have too much fun in school, that they don't believe in themselves or they don't appreciate the value of a dollar. We worry that they're being bullied, that they're bullying someone else, that they're falling behind educationally (when they're three years old), that they're not being challenged, that they will miss out on opportunities.

Parents also worry (a lot) that someone will snatch our children off the street. Most parents I know don't let their elementary-age kids go outside without supervision, even though we're all nostalgic for our own childhoods, when we spent entire days outside with our friends, watching for the street lights to come on or the sun to dip below the horizon—our signal that it was time to go home.

Many parents have a mental filmstrip constantly playing in the background of their minds, showing their children being abducted by strangers. They act in response to that visual imagery, sometimes taking protective steps that are unreasonable and which hamper kids' development of independence and self-confidence. Our national sense is that strangers are seizing children from their parents' protective custody all the time. In fact, while a real danger, this is a very uncommon event and a low risk if parents and children take sensible precautions.[3] And although we may have the sense that the world is a more dangerous place than it was when we didn't have the Internet and so many cable news channels available on TV, evidence indicates that such incidents have actually declined in recent years.

Crime statistics tell me I live in one of the absolute safest suburban ✓ communities in all of the Chicago metropolitan area. Not only that, but my community actually ranks among the safest in the entire state, scoring an 82 out of 100 on the safety scale. Yet I have trouble letting my thirteen-year-old daughter walk to the neighborhood park to hang out with her friends—two blocks away from our house and across the street from the home of some good family friends—without a cell phone. When I think about it, I have to acknowledge that if she is confronted with real danger—like a sudden attack by an abductor—the phone is unlikely to be of much use. I also have to acknowledge that if she faces a minor problem, she can easily seek help from her friends who are with her, alert the kind neighbors who live across the street from the park or walk two blocks home. Yet I irrationally insist on the phone simply to soothe my anxiety.

But worrying about their safety is not the only reason we keep our kids very close. In our current cultural climate, we parents find ourselves under social pressure to worry over our kids—and sometimes to express our worry through overprotection.

In 2008, mom and *New York Sun* columnist Lenore Skenazy wrote an article about allowing her nine-year-old son to ride the New York City subway by himself. She left him in Bloomingdale's, "gave him a subway map, a MetroCard, a $20 bill, and several quarters, just in case he had to make a call." He found his way home safely and with a new sense of his own capabilities, but Skenazy was publicly lambasted for her actions: "Half the people I've told this episode to now want to turn me in for child abuse." Her article started a national conversation on parental worry and overprotection, among people whose own generations were simply expected, as a matter of course, to develop this kind of independence as children.[4]

When you drive by a house where a child is playing alone in the front yard, is your first thought a celebration of that child's physical freedom and the parents' emotional freedom in allowing this kind of independence? Or do you wonder why no one cares about that child enough to keep her safely imprisoned behind closed doors? No one wants to be accused of bad parenting, especially those of us who already wonder if we're good enough. We are driven to more worry because we worry that if we don't worry about our kids, we'll be accused of neglect or apathy.

CIVIC WORRY

Concerned citizens worry about the economy, the education system, the health care system, the political system. We worry that the "right" candidates won't get elected, the "wrong" candidates will, things won't change, things will change, our fellow citizens won't care about what we care about, interest rates will increase, standards of living will decrease, we might not get ahead. We worry that our voices won't be heard, that our voices will be the only ones saying something unpopular, that our votes won't make a difference. We worry that we won't get what we need, that others will get something they didn't earn, that what we have will be taken away.

Worry actually seems to drive much of our political activity these days—especially every four years or so, when national elections remind us that the sky is still falling. We try to control the opinions of others, the outcomes of elections and cultural trends. We speculate on the Internet over the religious beliefs and hidden agendas of people in power. Some of us even watch hours of worried conversation among experts on television. And some waste two, four, six or eight years grating against the leaders God has ordained to positions of authority for his own purposes and called us to respect.

We worry that children are being left behind by school systems that can't possibly provide the kind of individual instruction we expect. Public school students get too much exposure to the world. Private school students get too little. And homeschool students get too much exposure to, well, themselves. We worry that our schools are failing and our children are falling behind in an undefined contest against an unnamed opponent that seems tremendously important.

When asked about the quality of public schools in the United States, in an annual Gallup poll, Americans consistently give schools a grade of C or below. However, when parents of school-age children are asked about the quality of their own children's schools, they consistently rate their schools much higher. In 2010, the most recent year for which data is available, 77 percent of parents gave their own children's schools grades of A or B. Only 18 percent of Americans gave that kind of grade to the overall public education system—79 percent gave it a C or lower.[5] It's a striking illustration of the gap between people's perceptions—probably shaped largely by mass media, political agendas and their own imaginations—and their experiences. Many parents are infected with a general sense of education anxiety that causes them to worry that their children won't receive a good education, but when acknowledging their own experience, what they actually know to be true, they apparently have little reason to worry.

TOO MUCH INFORMATION

Being informed citizens is easier than ever; unfortunately, it can also be hazardous to our mental health. In efforts to boost ratings and maintain our prone-to-wander attention, news media present several new things for us to worry about each day. One woman told me she refuses to watch the news because "it propagates worry. It feeds our fears." Another friend takes a different approach and refuses to turn away because she wants her theology to be realistic about the world we live in. It's hard to know which point to embrace on that strategic spectrum.

Broadcasters flash compelling headlines and teasers that encourage us to click on links or tune in to what they say, often with very little substance in the actual stories. "What killer may be lurking in your refrigerator? Find out on the 10 o'clock news," they say. Tune in for the actual story, and you might find out that if your milk is more than six months old, it could contain bacteria that will make you sick. That's the killer in your fridge. Now on to the next story about a cat and a dog who have forged a friendship against all odds.

Even when the stories do have substance, sensationalism can elicit an anxious response that actually keeps us from responding productively. For example, as I was reading about antibacterial soaps on the *Scientific American* website, I noticed this link pointing to a related story: "The Crisis of Antibiotic Resistance: Bacteria are finally overrunning our last defenses. Can we stop them?" When I clicked on the link, I saw that the story was accompanied by a picture of two people shaking hands, with one person's arm covered in sickly green dots—I assume meant to represent deadly bacteria.[6]

For many readers, this headline and photo will not prompt a reasonable, productive response that will move them to act sensibly on what they learn from reading the story. Instead, they will cause readers' hearts to beat a little faster and their eyes to widen in the face of what they're pretty sure is an oncoming train laden with malicious bacteria. For many people, it may not matter what the actual story says. The sensationalistic link and the photo will revisit them in the wee hours of the morning, when they lie sleepless in bed and resolve to buy more antibacterial soap to protect themselves from those horrible green bacteria on the people they shake hands with, thus compounding the problem. Our worry about disease feeds our appetite for sensational headlines about bacteria, which feed our compulsive pursuit of cleanliness, which feeds the risk of new kinds of disease, which feeds our worry.

Because our world has grown so small, news media present us with a lot of detailed information we can't realistically do much with. For example, I hear a lot about ongoing tensions in the Middle East, and I try to maintain a reasonable level of intelligence about what's happening in that part of the world. But I have yet to learn of any practical, productive, hands-on way to help in response to what I learn. And I've certainly never been moved to try to personally intervene in the ongoing tensions among people I don't know, in a conflict I don't understand, in a place where grievances predate the establishment of my own country by roughly four thousand years. So what am I to do with so much information? What can we do in response to such stories, which inundate us twenty-four hours a day, seven days a week if we tune in? We can pray, we can listen for ways our decisions affect the decisions people make in other parts of the world. We can try to persuade influential people to exercise their influence in the best possible way. But if that doesn't feel like enough—and to most of us it doesn't—we'll probably also incorporate the issue at hand into our regular regimen of worry.

Social Media

Social media has dramatically increased our ability to worry publicly over people and places we don't know, and to cause others to worry over them too. When one person with an influential voice sends a message highlighting an announcement, a cause or the plight of someone in need, that message can make its way to a vast audience in a matter of seconds. Suddenly millions of people receive alarming news, perhaps with horrifying images and very little context, usually with no guidance on how to respond meaningfully and helpfully. We don't even know whether what we're hearing or seeing is true.

When Hurricane Sandy hit the east coast of the United States in October 2012, millions of people emailed and reposted fake images supposedly depicting the storm's impact. One widely circulated image showed the Statue of Liberty in peril, nearly overcome by ocean waves. The picture was taken from a 2004 disaster movie. Another showed the statue under a swirl of dark, ominous clouds. The image was a product of Photoshop, using a storm chaser's photograph of a powerful storm that had formed over Nebraska eight years earlier. Regardless of their inaccuracy, these images appealed to many people's hunger just to know *something*. And most weren't content to keep the information to themselves—they passed it on.

Every week is a new campaign to "raise awareness" of frightening realities, often among people who are already quite aware of those realities. Our inboxes are full of spam emails, forwarded by people we respected until they got too much time on their hands and started sending a steady stream of alarmist messages, troublesome myths and nagging urban legends. Most of us are constantly fighting a battle to discern true information from false—and sometimes losing. We have access to more information than we can actually process, which comes at us at a pace and with a force we can't possibly absorb. One suburban mom told me she now understands the urge people feel to move to a place where they believe they can escape the technology-laced world "to separate their family from being bombarded with nonstop messages and unavoidable visuals."

When we receive such messages—real or not—designed to elicit a response, we feel as if something is expected of us and we should change something in our lives. So we go ahead and worry because we don't know what else to do, any calm response feels callous, and forgetting about what we read or saw is not an option.

Celebrity Causes

And lest we forget to pay attention to them amid the flood of information, celebrities keep their pet causes in front of us, using their influence to champion what's important to them and constantly telling us what we should worry over. Their personal campaigns reinforce their personal brands, so they receive plenty of publicity for their contributions to awareness. These campaigns usually contain little or no call to practical action aside from highlighting what the celebrities themselves do. Most of those interventions—meeting with world leaders, handpicking children from orphanages in fast-track adoptions, founding self-funding charities—are not available to the average person. So the rest of us are left with increased awareness of more causes that feel important enough to worry over but not accessible enough to help address.

MARKETING MESSAGES

A constant barrage of increasingly targeted marketing messages creates in us a sense of urgency about things that don't actually matter at all. Should we really be that concerned about whether women's deodorant is strong enough for a man? Do babies need an electric warmer to heat their wipes? Is it really important to kill 99.9 percent of germs on the *inside* of my toilet bowl? And just how white do my teeth need to be? I know there was a time when the world got along just fine without a special machine to cook grilled cheese sandwiches. And with blankets that didn't have sleeves.

INSURANCE INDUSTRY

People who have the most have the most reasons to worry about losing what they have. The insurance industry makes a lot of money capitalizing on our worry and our awareness of all the things that could go wrong along our journey through life. Responsible people, they tell us, are insured for every possibility, so adults need to make sure all the people and things that matter to them are fully covered. But while some forms and quantities of insurance are practical and necessary, others aren't. And despite what they may suggest, insurance companies aren't selling what we really want to buy: safety and security. We can never be certain anyone or anything is safe, no matter how much insurance we have.

LEGAL THREATS

In our litigious society, it has become natural to think about potential lawsuits and preemptively defend against them. The threat of ruinous legal action always looms, and organizations and some individuals spend a lot of energy worrying about whether their backsides are covered. That's how we ended up with containers of hand soap, hand lotion and topical acne medication that all say, "For external use only." That's why my insulated mug, designed to keep drinks hot, warns me that the liquid inside might be hot. And that's why I'm currently holding a bag of walnuts that says, "Processed in a facility which processes tree nuts" and a jar of peanut butter with a label warning "Contains peanuts."

Constant Choices

Speaking of products, have you ever stood in the cereal aisle or the drink aisle at a grocery store and tried to make sense of all the options? Buying water, milk and eggs requires making multiple choices. And forget about the bread aisle—nothing simple about that. Even selecting toilet paper can boggle the mind.

It doesn't stop with the grocery store. We are faced with choices all day, every day, sometimes with very little basis for making a selection. From what products we consume to what we wear, how to present ourselves, what music to listen to, what to watch on TV, what to read, which route to take to work, how to exercise and what to eat. We are so accustomed to this daily string of choices that most of us don't even realize how it drains us. From the time we rise to the time we fall asleep (if we're not awake in the night with anxiety), we make complex choices that tax our ability to relax, focus, be content, love God, love others and engage in the present moment.

In his book *The Paradox of Choice: Why More Is Less*, Barry Schwartz talks about why our dizzying array of choices is making us miserable: "Perhaps there comes a point at which opportunities become so numerous that we feel overwhelmed. Instead of feeling in control, we feel unable to cope. Having the opportunity to choose is no blessing if we feel we do not have the wherewithal to choose wisely."[7] A luxury of our age, the endless choices lead to constant decision making, which worries us and taxes our energies. It requires us to be "on" all the time, with our systems processing input, anticipating the future, trying to bring some measure of control to a world that feels like it's getting away from us. Our minds are groomed for worry.

We have so much to worry about. And if you aren't worried, the world around you will assume you are uncaring, emotionally dead, unengaged in the human experience and unproductive. Worry is fashionable.

GOOD CHRISTIAN WORRY

My experience tells me that most Christians are as worried as everyone else, and as convinced that a certain amount of worry is a good thing. We actually seem proud of our anxiety—again, as long as it doesn't become "excessive." And as long as it doesn't betray a lack of trust in God over the big things.

Here are some ways our Christian culture expects us to worry.

Display of dedication. We worry out loud to show that we're responsible and engaged in doing things that matter. We say things that remind me of Prince Humperdinck, the villainous ruler in the classic movie *The Princess Bride*. When asked if he wants to watch the torture of his rival Wesley, he arrogantly tells Count Rugen, "Tyrone, you know how much I love watching you work, but I've got my country's 500th anniversary to plan, my wedding to arrange, my wife to murder and Guilder to frame for it; I'm swamped." We talk about our demands at work, family responsibilities, personal commitments and goals not because the people around us are especially interested in the details, but because we want our worry to prove that we're working hard, that we're not slackers, that we're busy doing the work Christians should do.

Worried prayers. We worry in our prayer requests to show we care. "I'm really worried about Danny. He needs our prayers." We sometimes worry in our actual prayers too, not really praying but simply reciting our worries to God without surrender or faith. We bring our requests to God and tell him all about what's weighing on us, worrying before him, then walk away and continue to worry, hoping God is worried too, now that we've filled him in, but also worrying that he won't resolve our concerns in the way we hope for. We're often missing the step of allowing prayer to settle us back into our appropriate place in the universe, affirming God's sovereignty and trusting him.

Communicating our calling. We talk about what's "keeping us up at night" as proof that we have important things going on in our lives, that God has called us to significant responsibilities. In gatherings of pastors and leaders of Christian organizations, I often hear this used as a discussion question or icebreaker: "What's keeping you up at night?" The assumption is that we are all losing sleep because God has made us important. I've wondered how it would go over to say, "I'm not losing sleep. God has given me the gift of his peace, and he has assured me that he is capable of running the world while I'm asleep." I imagine this response meeting with suspicion, not celebration.

The church's future. We wring our hands over the sorry condition of our youth and the bleak future of the church. When I was growing up in the church as a child, I remember hearing a lot about the dreadful state of young people. When I became a teenager myself, I heard the same messages about my own age group, infused with a lot of angst over whether we could possibly endure life among the pressures we faced. I remember thinking adults had a pretty low opinion of our ability to navigate a world that was native to us.

When I became an adult, I began hearing about a new generation of young people who thought in alarming new ways and probably would abandon the church completely. I've now been around long enough to realize that this worry about the next generation is constant. Only the specific cultural culprits change. As trends shift our culture, our mistrust of the generations who come after us, coupled with our emotional investment in the future of the world, can lead to a mistrust of God's ability to work in new generations. In turn, it can lead us to believe our worried oversight is necessary to keep the whole church from falling apart once we're gone.

Evangelistic worry. We wring our hands over the potential fate of nonbelievers. We call this "a burden for the lost," even though it can go way beyond what might legitimately be called by that name. Some Christians have lost sight of the Holy Spirit's role and the fact that salvation is actually God's work. We are blessed to embody Jesus' presence in this world, and called to be his witnesses, but not expected to do what is his work alone. Because we cannot do God's job (although many try), some of us do an awful lot of worrying when we figure he is not doing it well enough.

Moral reaction. We worry over the state of our world and its morality, seemingly surprised that the effects of cumulative sin have created a less-than-ideal place with serious systemic problems. Christian leaders establish organizations and public platforms dedicated to railing against the behavior of the world around us. The misguided nature of this is implied in the words of the apostle Paul: "It isn't my responsibility to judge outsiders, but it certainly is your responsibility to judge those inside the church who are sinning. God will judge those on the outside; but as the Scriptures say, 'You must remove the evil person from among you'" (1 Cor 5:12-13).

Why are we so surprised to see the world around us looking like a world full of sin? We are called to be salt and light to the world, not to condemn it—even Jesus said he didn't come to do that—or to worry over God's job of judgment. Some of us seem to believe it's our responsibility to change the behavior of people who live in spiritual darkness. Taking on this burden can mean a lot of worry because there's very little action we can take, and ultimately our judgmental efforts are bound to be unsuccessful.

Saving the world. Especially in younger generations, Christians exert a lot of energy worrying about people who live in poverty, in nations decimated by ongoing war and in cultures with oppressive practices. With a growing sense of awareness and compassion for the world beyond our doors, it is unacceptable to behave as if we are callous to those needs. So we feel an urgency to show we care—even though most of us don't even understand what the real problems are, let alone how we can help. In reality, there are not a lot of practical and immediate ways most of us can change these harsh realities; our most effective role usually means supporting those who are engaged at a direct and much deeper level. At the same time, most of us feel as if there must be more we should do. So we translate our energy into worry, just to show we're not hiding out in a comfortable Christian bubble.

Worry Is a Problem

Because worry is so pervasively embedded in our culture and our daily experience, it's easy to dismiss it as benign, when done in moderation, or simply as a widespread bad habit. It's socially acceptable even among Christians who occasionally become aware that our worry is excessive and sort of apologize for it without repentance: "I know I shouldn't worry so much."

Yet we are called to live and think differently. The fact is, worry is destructive. And a look through Scripture shows us that worry is sinful—a rebellious activity that creates distance between us and God. Voluntary worry grows from a spiritual problem, which ultimately cannot be overcome merely through an act of the will—the solution is rooted entirely in who God is. God has repeatedly told us not to worry, not only in the well-known words of Jesus recorded in Matthew 6 but also throughout the Old Testament and in the Epistles to the early church. (See chapter four for an exploration of several of these passages.)

We say we know we shouldn't worry, but we don't seem to give much thought to why worry offends God. Yet understanding the theology of worry is critical to true transformation. And I hope, as we think that through, it will encourage you to turn away from worry—an activity that is destructive not only "in excess" as our culture defines it, but in any amount.

BE TRANSFORMED

Rejecting worry starts with recognizing why worry offends God and accepting our proper relationship to him, to the future, and to the people and things he has placed in our care. Then we must practice doing what he has told us to do.

So if you're worried, as many of us are, and you want to change that habit, how do you do that? You can try to just stop worrying, but simply changing a behavior doesn't address the true source of the problem. For real and lasting change, you also need to "let God transform you into a new person by changing the way you think" (Rom 12:2). Of course, that transformative process is conducted and guided by God and his Holy Spirit, not by us. But we can choose to welcome and cooperate with that work, or we can choose to fear, resent and resist it.

We can be transformed not just because we choose to behave differently, but because God changes our very hearts and minds. And as our mindsets change, our behavior will too. As you seek to welcome this process of transformation in your life, try making yourself more receptive to God's influence. Surround and saturate yourself with the truth about God: who he is and why he is trustworthy and who you are in relationship to him. Ask God to change the way you think about him, about yourself, about everything. He loves to do this sort of thing, so get ready.

As you understand more of who God is and how he reveals himself to us, another important step is necessary: you must believe what God says. This is much easier said than done. Even though we believe in God and theoretically believe he is all-powerful and loving, sometimes it's hard to really believe he is in control of the world we live in, he will never leave us and the people we love, he is aware of absolutely everything we need and capable of providing it, he knows us better than we know ourselves, he is far more powerful than absolutely everything and everyone who scares us, and he has a great plan and a great view of realms and reasons we can't even imagine. Our lack of belief shows itself in our lives when we behave as if everything is up to us.

Everything is not up to us, and we can take some practical steps to show that we accept our limitations. Some of our worry is fueled by overcommitment. How can you downsize your calendar and release yourself from obligations that aren't truly important or that others are better suited for? Try to live at a pace that's reasonable for the temperament, energy level and responsibilities God has given you, with built-in margin so you can accommodate the unexpected and avoid constant time pressure.

My friend Nancy started a blog called *The Good Enough Mom.* I love that name and the attitude behind it. More of us would live and love better if we pronounced "good enough" over the parts of our lives that cause chronic dissatisfaction. Much of our worry is fueled by our attempts to keep up with the people around us, to achieve impossible standards. Go ahead and embrace disappointment; you'll never get there. As long as you're looking around for people to emulate, you'll never be as rich, good-looking, knowledgeable, cultured, fashionable, strong, successful, capable, amusing, popular, self-disciplined, trendy, creative, informed, powerful or happy as you feel you should be. So let go and be yourself.

As Mary did on the occasion described in Luke 10:38-42, we must choose the "one thing worth being concerned about." What is it? Devotion to Jesus.

It's important that we admit our powerlessness against much of what worries us. People often speak of "giving it over to God," essentially asking him to take over management of things we've been working on after we've flubbed them up. This idea is a bit of a charade. We don't really have the power to assign work to God. Admitting our powerlessness is not really about handing things over to God as much as acknowledging what is already true—he already holds these things that worry us. We don't truly have the power to give them or take them away from him. It's an illusion. The future is already his, and all power belongs to him.

Do you really trust God? Do you believe that he is always good and that he always acts in your best interest (by his definition), for his glory? That he is more powerful than you can imagine, so powerful that he "laid the foundations of the earth" (Job 38:4)? See appendix B in this book for some inspiration, and ask God to grant you faith to believe.

Next let's take a closer look at just what worry is, how we express it and how it hurts us. You may be worrying more than you realize.

3

Worry's Many
Destructive Powers

So is all this worry helping us? Perhaps it helps when the discomfort of anxiety motivates us to do something about it. As my friend Deb pointed out, worry can make us aware of what's really bothering us. Once we identify the problem, we can channel our energy into doing something productive. Another friend told me that worry sometimes motivates him to think things through more thoroughly. But in both cases, the true motivation is likely coming from a desire to relieve worry, not from the worry itself. And a positive outcome demands we move on from worry to something healthier.

Does worry itself make us more productive? At times, perhaps. In general, probably not. Constant mental activity and physical tension—even physical movement—don't necessarily translate into productive action. In fact, one might argue that because it keeps our minds and bodies in a state of high alert, mentally rehearsing possibilities and if-onlys, worry inhibits our productivity by keeping us from the strengthening rest we need. We are not made to function effectively for long periods of time in a state of anxiety.

Still not convinced worry is a problem in your life? Perhaps you're thinking too small.

HOW WE HURT OURSELVES WITH WORRY

There is more than one way to worry. When we're worried, we may not even be aware of all the ways worry is expressing itself in our behavior. And we may not realize just how much it's hurting us.

Obsession. A worried mind races and wrestles, trying to find a new perspective on a problem or a possibility that no amount of thinking will unravel. Like the infamous Grinch, who "puzzled and puzzled 'till his puzzler was sore,"[1] we seem to believe that with enough thought, everything that weighs on us will become clear, manageable or avoidable. The problem is, much of what we worry about is outside our control or hasn't even happened. Often we're trying to solve problems that don't yet exist.

For some of us, worry feels better when we do it aloud. Talking about our worries with others, we can express them in a new way and pull others into the experience with us. The upside to talking about our worries is that they sometimes grow smaller in the light of someone else's perspective, or we get a more objective view when we hear them coming out of our mouths. The downside: sometimes they grow larger with reinforcement from the person we're talking to. Most of the time, they don't change at all—we just run over the same ground like a rodent on a wheel, squeaking away with no productive result.

Many of us like to worry in groups. We seek others who will affirm that we're worrying about the right things and who will worry right alongside us. We may start out seeking comfort and emotional support, only to find ourselves wallowing in the same place, but now with company. Everyone else feels pressure to join in, and pretty soon we're all worrying in concert.

Worry is not only a condition of the mind and the mouth; it can be a condition of the body as well. Some worried people can't sit still. Because their minds are restless, they can't feel comfortable with their bodies at rest, so they stay in constant motion even when it's unnecessary. The worried parent paces the living room floor when a teenage son or daughter misses curfew. The nervous son or daughter who missed curfew starts chewing fingernails. The anxious employee taps her feet and twirls her pen through her fingers during a tense meeting. The high-strung woman moves from one housekeeping task to the next, wishing for a break but not daring to stop. The tense man keeps his fingers tapping away at the keyboard on his laptop while he watches a movie with his wife. We worry through pointless and unproductive activity, trying to just stay busy and to increase our sense of control.

Many people are slaves to the double-check. As soon as we leave the house, we start to wonder whether we turned off the oven. When we lie down at night, we wonder if the doors really are locked—even though we just locked them. When we don't receive timely responses to our emails, we check to make sure we really sent them, even though we know we did. Even though my kids are in their preteen and teenage years, I still can't go to bed without first checking to make sure they're still breathing—a habit I developed when they were newborns.

If the oven or the iron might be on or the front door might be open, it makes sense to check. But often, we go through this ritual even though we know there's no reason to check again. Rationally, we know the doors are locked, but we want to soothe ourselves. A worried thought habitually enters our heads, and we give in to it to achieve peace of mind. And then we check again.

Like other obsessions, worry tends to consume us. It will take as much of us as we're willing to give. Sometimes when we worry, we develop a hyper-focus on one issue, neglecting other matters that should have some of our attention.

One Sunday morning, I saw such obsession in action as I was serving as a substitute small-group leader for a group of elementary-age girls. I was fairly new to the church, and I didn't know any of the kids in the group. I had never met their regular small-group leader, and I didn't know why she needed a substitute that week—I had just volunteered to help.

As the girls arrived, I introduced myself to each of them and told them I was filling in for their regular group leader that week. Even though they were meeting me for the first time, most of the kids were fine with this change in their routine. But one girl was really troubled by the absence of their usual leader, Jana. She asked me why Jana was gone that week, and my honest answer ("I don't know") didn't help. As I attempted to lead them through some activities and discussion, this poor girl remained so fixated on the missing Jana that she was completely unable to engage in what the rest of the group was doing. I spent half the meeting time assuring her that Jana was fine and would be back in the future (while fervently praying that was true, since I didn't really know). Eventually she relaxed enough to participate, but she never fully focused on the lesson at hand. The rest of the group, too, was distracted by this obsession and, I fear, went home thinking more about "The Mystery of the Missing Jana" than about what I had tried to help them learn that day.

When possibilities peek over the horizon, some of us express our obsession by gathering as much information as we can. The Consumer Confidence Index fell by half a point? Research the possible economic trends that might be underway. Your boss looked nervous today? Speculate with your coworkers over what it means. Little Jacob has a fever? Go online and find out what diseases he might be developing. Check his symptoms and follow the trail into an informational black hole, working your way through one possibility after another until you look up to find an hour has passed and your hands are shaking over the thought of some rare disease with no cure.

We have so much information available to us—nearly limitless amounts for those motivated to find it. When questions arise, we have grown accustomed to quickly finding or knowing who to ask about just about anything we want to learn. So when we find ourselves confronting what we truly can't know—like future outcomes—it's only natural for us to express our worry by seeking answers in the same ways we usually do. But despite all our obsessing, mysteries persist and the future remains undocumented.

Unfortunately, worry doesn't always act as a motivator. It often acts more like tar, keeping us stuck in indecision and even emotional or mental paralysis. Deb said, "I think worry can be hurtful to me. It can be second-guessing myself. This can result in distractions, loss of focus, wasted time and frustration."

When we become obsessed with worry, we may have trouble moving past it, or even seeing past it to what might come next. In this sense, worry is not only unproductive, but also counterproductive—actually preventing us from positive action.

Control issues. Worry reinforces the idea that everything is up to us. That idea causes more worry, which fuels a false sense of responsibility, which gives birth to a gigantic desire for control. After all, without control over our circumstances and the people around us, how can we possibly fulfill our responsibility to make sure everything happens as it should?

One friend told me, "When I worry, it's only because I'm taking on myself something that I'm not willing to give up control of. There's a fine line between figuring out something that I need to plan and be discerning about, and worrying about something. I pray often for God's wisdom to make that distinction."

One man said, "I think I worry because I want to better control a situation that is on the brink of spinning out of control, or at least in a direction that I am not comfortable going."

We worry about losing control, about how to exert or maintain control. We worry about how to get out from under others' control; how to gain the upper hand in our relationships; how to control people like our kids, our employees and our elected representatives. We try to anticipate circumstances that may flatten us, and lie awake at night plotting ways to change those circumstances. We feel a disturbing sense that we can't control everything we want to, and that scares us. Sometimes worry provides a way to feel as if we are moving closer to the kind of control that will soothe us.

We are creatures of tremendous imaginative ability (some more than others), and not much imagination is required to envision bad things happening to us. Reality being what it is, we can easily picture tragedies hurting the people we love, threatening the things we hold dear and making the world an even more dangerous place. When we allow our minds to dwell on possibilities, we can find plenty of reasons to worry. We live in a world where suffering is inescapable.

We sometimes worry in misguided attempts at prevention, as if worrying about the bad things that might happen will somehow ward them off. When I asked several people about their worries, common responses included several that suggested preventive worry: health, family safety, losing a job, the future condition of our country and our world.

This kind of worry is futile, of course, and serves only to heap imaginary misery on the burdens of today. We don't have this kind of control. As sixteenth-century French writer Michel de Montaigne put it, "My life has been full of terrible misfortunes, most of which never happened." He also said, "A man who fears suffering is already suffering from what he fears."

Speaking of suffering, we all want to help people who are hurting and in need. People with strong empathetic streaks are especially burdened by the needs of others. But we're all aware of more hardship than we can possibly relieve. The frustrating truth is, sometimes we can't do anything to help. And sometimes the ways we can help don't feel like enough. This truth doesn't sit well with can-do, capable people who are socialized to believe every problem has a solution and nearly every solution is within reach. When we feel the frustration of helplessness, we figure there must be something we can do. And when our minds cast out for that solution, they often land on worry.

When we can't do anything else, we can worry. Sometimes worry is a way of trying to do something about a situation we honestly can't do much about.

When I was in graduate school learning about how people work in teams, I had to take a test to assess my locus of control. In personality theory, each of us has a perceived locus of control—the place where we believe our circumstances are determined. That sense of control can lie either internally (within our own actions and choices) or externally (with other people or with God, fate, or some other power). People with a high internal locus of control believe they are responsible, at least in part, for most of what happens to them. Conversely, people with a high external locus of control believe other forces are largely responsible for their circumstances and even their own choices. So when two people start businesses that succeed, the person with a high internal locus of control will believe the success comes from his or her own business acumen and smart choices. The person with the high external locus of control will believe customers are generous or market forces smile on them. And when those same two people fail in business, the person with the high internal locus of control will attribute the failure to his or her own bad business decisions. The other person will figure the market went soft or "it just wasn't meant to be."

I had never heard of locus-of-control theory before that class, and I was fascinated by what the assessment revealed about me: I had an extremely high internal locus of control, the highest in my class of MBA students. Apparently I really did think everything was up to me.

I haven't taken this assessment again, but I hope that if I did, I would achieve a score closer to balance. In the years since, I have learned to acknowledge more of my limitations and let go of some of the things I felt I had to take responsibility for. While people with a high internal locus of control tend to be high achievers and influencers, extremism on this scale is not truly healthy. It fails to reflect reality. We are responsible for ourselves and the influence we exert around us—but we are not responsible for other people's choices, and we are always subject to God's authority. People who desire more control than they've been granted are prime candidates for repeated disappointment and ongoing frustration—not to mention relational friction. The more we worry, the more we reinforce the idea that the objects of our worry are our responsibility and should be under our control.

Future fears. Perhaps the most common type of worry is also the most comically futile. It's the effort to live where we do not live—in the future. The future is full of promise and terror. If everything we fear about the future were to happen, none of us would be here.

In 1900, a writer named John Elfreth Watkins Jr. wrote an article for the *Ladies' Home Journal* detailing his predictions for the year 2000. Among his twenty-nine predictions, some were startlingly accurate; others were roughly on the right track. But some were laughably erroneous. For example, he predicted that "mosquitoes, house-flies and roaches will have been practically exterminated. . . . There will be no wild animals except in menageries. Rats and mice will have been exterminated. The horse will have become practically extinct." He also felt people would become so much stronger, "a man or woman unable to walk ten miles at a stretch will be regarded as a weakling." He envisioned that "food will be served hot or cold to private houses in pneumatic tubes. . . . The meal being over, the dishes used will be packed and returned to the cooking establishments where they will be washed. . . . These tubes will collect, deliver and transport mail over certain distances, perhaps for hundreds of miles."[2]

Watkins made his predictions based on the information and trends he could see at the time. He never could have predicted everything that the twentieth century would bring. I wish he had been right about the mosquitoes, but unfortunately even the most sensible predictions are constrained by our own limitations. We simply can't see the future, can't live in it and, in a sense, can't even find it—it's always at least a day away (as the irrepressible Annie would say). And we have no guarantee that we'll live to see tomorrow.

Given our limitations, worry about the future carries a certain absurdity. Yet it casts a menacing shadow over today, demanding attention and tempting us in our tendency to reject our limitations. So we let the unknown tomorrows rule us today, despite the unlikelihood that we'll ever find ourselves in the precise future we imagine.

In my conversations with others, the unknown future was the number-one source of worry people mentioned. Cory said, "What causes the most worry is my future. I'm in my mid-thirties and single, and at my lowest times I struggle with a fear of being alone, which then leads to my questioning God and having a low self-image, stripping away my joy and peace."

One woman said, "I like to know what's coming, so if I don't, I find myself wasting time and energy on trying to figure out how things can work out. I've learned that I have to stop trying to plan it all. Circumstances change or something unexpected happens, and my contemplating and worrying were for nothing."

The future belongs to God, not us, and when we try to live in it, we only create more trouble for today. (More on this in chapter 6.)

Physical suffering. Remember the fear response I described in chapter one: among other effects, the heart and lungs move faster, muscles tense, the skin flushes or grows pale, the pupils dilate, and the senses may become either dulled or hyperalert. When the body and brain immediately respond to fear in these ways, we have what we need to fight or flee danger—this response helps us. But when the body and brain stay fixated in this state, we suffer.

Few would be surprised to learn that the majority of Americans say they live under moderate to high stress levels. This constant stress has many consequences for our health, including high blood pressure, obesity, sleeplessness, fatigue, headaches, depression and digestion problems. In a 2010 survey by the American Psychological Association, 40 percent of people said that in the past month, stress had caused them to overeat or to eat unhealthy foods. Nearly one-third said they had skipped a meal because of stress, and more than 25 percent said they had been unable to sleep. "The most common physical symptoms of stress reported were irritability (45 percent), fatigue (41 percent) and lack of energy or motivation (38 percent)."[3] Another study affirmed that worry has a negative impact on heart function.[4]

Worry can cause shortness of breath; heart palpitations; pain and damage in the back, neck, and shoulders; muscle tension; nausea; headaches and other problems.[5] When I asked people about their experiences with worry, one person mentioned suffering from a "churning stomach." Another talked about his problems with acid reflux, stress headaches and back pain. Many of us have come to expect such worry-related aches and pains as normal, part of the wallpaper in our lives.

A couple of years ago, I sprained an ankle and went on with life as if nothing had happened. This took place during a hectic and stressful time, when my husband and I were both in the midst of job transitions, our oldest daughter was starting middle school, and we were offering support to my sister and our brother-in-law, who recently had been diagnosed with stage 3 liver cancer and needed a transplant. My mind was preoccupied, my body was busy and I didn't have space in my life for an injury. So I hobbled around and kept aggravating the sprain, while my mind stubbornly refused to register the level of pain I was experiencing. I didn't even look at my ankle for three weeks. Finally, I was forced to slow down when I tried to navigate a corn maze with my kids and couldn't walk on the uneven ground. When I sat down and actually looked at the ankle, I saw that it was swollen and discolored and realized I needed to take care of it. So I did, but it took months to heal. And now, because I waited so long to treat it, I have ongoing trouble with that ankle, the consequence of my neglect.

Our amazing minds can focus on one set of problems to the exclusion of others. This can be helpful when a problem or task demands our full attention for a short time. But when we allow our minds to fixate on worry—a waste of time and energy—we may overlook the legitimate demands of our bodies and souls. We may not be as vigilant about what we eat, may forgo exercise, may even neglect basic hygiene.

Beyond physical pain, bad habits and a decrease in quality of life, worry can actually make us sick. It can suppress our immune systems, making us more vulnerable to all kinds of illnesses. Over time, it can cause digestive disorders, premature coronary artery disease and heart attacks.[6] Thus, the expression "worried sick."

When forty-three-year-old political commentator Andrew Breitbart died of heart failure in 2012, many people wondered whether his high-stress, revved-up emotional style contributed to his death. Bloggers pointed out that Breitbart was known for an animated, angry disposition, prone to arguing and yelling. At least in his public persona, he appeared to carry the weight of the world—as he saw it—on his shoulders. This weight, some think, actually killed him. Whether this theory is unfounded or not, it shows that we know, intuitively, that worry isn't good for us.

Mental illness. Prolonged worry can cause illness not only in our bodies but also in our minds. Chronic worry can create a hospitable environment for anxiety disorders. It can also lead to depression and thoughts of suicide.[7] In the words of Dr. Edward Hallowell:

> At its worst, worry is insidious, invisible, a relentless scavenger, roaming the corners of your mind, feeding on anything it finds. It sets upon you unwanted and unbidden, feasting on the infinite array of negative possibilities in life, diminishing your enjoyment of friends, family, achievements, and physical being—all because you live in fear of what might go wrong. People who worry too much suffer. For all their hard work, for all their

humor and willingness to laugh at themselves, for all their self-awareness, worriers just cannot achieve peace of mind.[8]

In any twelve-month period, 18 percent of adults in the United States experience an anxiety disorder that significantly impairs their ability to function in everyday life. Over the course of a lifetime, 29 percent of us will experience such an anxiety disorder. And this is not an issue only for adults. The average age of onset for anxiety disorders is eleven years old.[9]

Six million people in the United States suffer from panic disorder, a condition characterized by sudden and unpredictable panic attacks. People with panic disorder are sometimes overwhelmed and debilitated by terror and its accompanying physical symptoms as fear-related chemicals surge through their bodies.[10]

Mental illness has many faces and many causes; I am not suggesting that all mental illness is caused by worry or other thought patterns. Most mental illness has its origin in a complex mix of genetics, environment, experiences, personal choices and factors that remain mysterious to medical professionals. We cannot legitimately blame people for developing mental illnesses because they "worry too much." But we can say that our own choices, the ways we care for ourselves and respond to our circumstances, and the habitual thought patterns we develop can make us more susceptible to disorders. And habitual worry can welcome and nurture the growth of anxiety-related malfunction. (For more on this, see appendix A in this book, "A Word About Anxiety Disorders.")

Sleeplessness. I'm a natural night owl, and falling asleep quickly does not come easily for me. When I'm worried, I find it difficult to fall asleep at all, even if I'm very tired. My husband, Trevor, is the opposite. He falls asleep mid-sentence, sometimes before his head hits the pillow. But while he's not particularly prone to worry in general, he occasionally wakes in the early hours of the morning with stressful thoughts, plans and possibilities running through his mind. Some nights, we inadvertently run a nightlong worry vigil, with me covering the first few hours and him covering the rest. My husband and I are not unusual. Worry is not the only reason people find themselves lying awake at night, but it is common. In one survey conducted by the American Psychological Association, 44 percent of adults indicated that stress had caused them to lie awake at night at least once in the previous month.[11] As Westerners struggling to keep pace in an accelerating world, we tend to underrate the value of sleep and overrate our own abilities to go without it. Contrary to what we may believe, besides frustrating nights and drowsy days, sleeplessness can have serious consequences.

No one really knows why, but sleep is critical to the proper functioning of our bodies and minds. Studies show that sleep deficits slow our thinking, compromise memory, make learning difficult, impair our reaction time, cause irritability, increase anger, decrease capacity for stress and make us less likely to engage in good habits such as eating well and exercising.[12] Sleeplessness also increases the risk of depression and anxiety. In one study conducted by the University of North Texas, people with insomnia were almost ten times more likely to suffer from clinical depression and more than seventeen times more likely to be affected by "clinically significant" anxiety.[13]

Sleeplessness affects our judgment and concentration[14] and is linked with higher levels of substance abuse. It is also linked with a heightened risk of driving accidents, obesity, diabetes and heart problems.[15]

Experts say sleep needs vary somewhat from person to person, but according to the National Sleep Foundation, most adults need seven to nine hours of sleep each night.[16] By contrast, American adults average less than seven hours of sleep. And nearly two-thirds (63 percent) say their sleep needs are not met during the week.[17]

Obviously, many of us don't get enough sleep on the best of nights, so we certainly can't afford to battle insomnia. But sometimes we just can't let go of the opportunity to worry and try to solve what's bothering us. We refuse rest, as if the world will fall apart without our vigilance. When we feel overwhelmed by what worries us, we tend not to go to bed when we should because it would mean letting go of some control, acknowledging that our worry isn't helpful and believing that the future of the world doesn't depend on our staying awake. And when worried people do go to bed, we often lie awake. But losing sleep only compounds our problems.

Self-abuse. When we're worried or filled with other negative emotions, many of us try to soothe ourselves with food, alcohol, drugs, shopping and other forms of consumption. We aren't sure what to do with all the mental and emotional energy that comes from keeping our systems at the ready, so we channel it into activities that will help us express that energy and bring us pleasure at the same time.

An extreme example of this is hoarding behavior, which is associated with obsessive-compulsive disorder, a severe anxiety disorder. Although most of us would not classify as hoarders, many of us do seek the transient pleasure that comes from acquiring, owning and ingesting what we want. Instead of resolving our worries, as productive action might, such behaviors create more anxiety as we deal with their consequences.

Many of us go beyond unhealthy consumption to actual abuse of ourselves. Worry is uncomfortable. Anxiety demands relief. When we're consumed by the feelings they induce, human nature drives us to seek relief in the fastest, easiest ways we can. But sometimes these comforts are really bad for us.

It makes sense that someone in a high-anxiety state might desire the short-term succor of a depressant like alcohol, a soothing drug like marijuana, an opiate like oxycodone or a sedative. The tragedy is that the long-term effects of these substances are never helpful. They don't make problems go away; they actually introduce new troubles. For example, according to one study, people who drink alcohol as a way to soothe their anxieties are more likely to develop social phobia and alcohol addictions. In this study, people who self-medicated with alcohol to address an anxiety disorder were two to five times more likely to develop an alcohol problem within three years compared to people who did not self-medicate. They were also more likely to develop social phobia or social anxiety disorder.[18]

Alcohol and drugs aren't the only options for short-term self-soothing. Many people seek comfort in food, sex, self-injury (such as cutting), shopping, social networking, entertainment and fantasy. No amount of crème brûlée, expensive shoes or fantastic sex will make our problems go away or train our brains to rest in trust instead of worry. These choices all fail to provide long-term solutions to our troubles.

There's a special kind of cruel irony in this reality: some of the most tantalizing sources of easy comfort come at an incredible price and never fail to compound our trouble with more reasons to worry.

Emotional pain. Worry saps our energy for life and our enjoyment of what God has given us. Many of us are so worried about future possibilities that we are completely missing opportunities for spiritual fulfillment and meaning in our lives now.

When someone in my family goes for a walk or a run, we usually include our energetic Lab mix, Rosie. But occasionally, for one reason or another, she's left behind. One scorching Saturday last summer, my husband and my daughter decided to go running in the middle of the day. The heat was too much for our black-coated dog, so they left her at home. I stayed behind too, and I invited her to cuddle with me on the couch.

Instead, Rosie, who was very upset at being left behind, spent the entire time they were gone pacing and whining in front of the door. She accomplished nothing but agitating herself and annoying me. She missed out on a chance to cuddle, nap, play, eat or run around the backyard. I tried distracting her with toys, treats and scratches behind the ears, but she couldn't enjoy any of that. All she could think about was missing out on a run—and she couldn't do anything about it.

Like Rosie, many of us miss out on the joys we might otherwise find right in front of us because we're completely focused on what worries us. Often, our worries aren't even present realities; they're future possibilities. And while we're mentally living in a frightening future, the present sits unseen and unappreciated. Even in painful circumstances and moments of grief, God grants his people the gift of joy in his presence and in what he has made. But instead of enjoying his gifts, we mentally pace and whine in front of the door, longing to control our circumstances or determine the future.

Ironically, sometimes we worry in an effort to make us less worried. We try to calm our insecurities, convincing ourselves that we're more valuable, loved or safe than we feel. Worrying about important things can make us feel important. Worrying to people we love might convince them to assure us of their love in return. And worrying about the future might end in a reassuring realization that we don't have anything to worry about. Running through possibilities and weighing their likelihood, we hope to arrive at conclusions that will ease our minds. We want to soothe our troubling emotions, but ultimately, worry betrays us. No solution is ever foolproof or impervious to follow-up questions. Every path our worry leads us down opens onto three more paths, all covered in the same thorns.

People who live in worry lose sight of hope. They accept a sense of dread as their overwhelming orientation. They forget that our living, loving, personal, all-powerful God has a plan that can't be thwarted and offers us hope that doesn't waver. Focusing on worry seems to block the view of hope's march through history and its inevitable journey into the future.

There's usually some truth to what worries us (yes, those bad things really could happen; yes, terrible things are happening all over the world), but worry never tells the whole truth. The whole truth includes what God is doing, his power, the beauty in this world, the surprising kindness of sin-riddled people, our mysterious ability to endure far more than we're prepared for and the fact that I'm not responsible for how everything turns out.

A worried person is not emotionally positioned to delight in interactions with others. Worry robs experiences of their potential for growth and saps our interest in other people. Worry is an enemy of peace, confidence and contentment. A mind fixed on worry is not at rest. It's not receptive to what God says. A person who is expending energy on worry is unable to fully enter the experience of living under the influence of God's Holy Spirit: "love, joy, peace, patience, kindness, goodness, faithfulness, gentleness, and self-control" (Gal 5:22-23). And even if we go through the motions of spiritually sustaining activities such as church attendance, Bible reading and prayer, we can't fully engage in our own growth when distracted by worry.

Relational pain. One study found, not surprisingly, that "worrying can become so obsessive that it interferes with a person's life and damages social relationships."[19] Worry changes our mood, which in turn affects our relationships. Marriages and friendships suffer as people argue more, demand more of one another or withdraw from relationships. When we're worried, we may focus so thoroughly on our own emotions, impulses and thoughts that we can't properly participate in anything else. The process of worrying feels so important, we withdraw from others and live in our own heads, effectively ignoring the people we love and responsibilities that need our attention.

Worry can also mean withdrawing from our own physical needs and our responsibilities to ourselves. Sometimes worried people forget to eat and stop taking good care of themselves. They ignore family relationships and friendships. They neglect spiritual practices and communion with God. This usually means unintentionally burdening others with what should be our own self-care, all in favor of worry.

This kind of worry reminds me of the character Gollum in J. R. R.

Tolkien's *The Hobbit* and *The Lord of the Rings*. Gollum, who once was a hobbit known as Sméagol, found a powerful ring and lost himself to its allure. Although he never understood what he had found, he became obsessed with his precious ring and allowed it to consume him. He withdrew from everyone and everything he had known, hiding in caves and eventually forgetting who he was. He was destroyed by his obsession, yet he couldn't let it go.

When we worry, our own thoughts become so precious to us, we hold on to them at the expense of what we claim is most important to us. Parent-child relationships suffer. An American Psychological Association survey found that among children eight to seventeen years old, one-third believe their parents have been "always or often worried or stressed out" in the past month. Forty percent of children said they feel sad when their parents are worried or stressed, and children say they know their parents are stressed when they are yelling, arguing, complaining and neglecting to spend time with their kids. In this study, parents tended to dramatically underestimate the impact their own stress and worry have on their kids.[20]

When I asked people about their experiences with worry, I heard a lot about their relationships. Leanne said, "Unfortunately, when I let worry win over my emotions, it manifests itself as displaced aggression. I find that I'll lash out at my husband or sometimes even my kids for the little things they've done or not done. They have no way of knowing that I'm actually stressed out about something unrelated to them, and then on top of the anxiousness, I end up feeling guilty too!"

One of my friends mentioned that worry causes marital conflict, impatience and moodiness. Another woman talked about getting short-tempered when she's worried, and sometimes overreacting or saying things she doesn't mean. One man said when he's worried about work or trying to balance too much, he has to prevent himself from being short-tempered with others or appearing too busy to pour into a relationship.

Sometimes rather than causing us to distance ourselves from others, our worry causes us suffocate them. We hover over our employees, our coworkers, our children, our friends. Some of us micromanage doctors, dentists and teachers who care for our families. Behind this kind of worry is the sense that we know better than others do, we can do things better than they can and everything will fall apart if we leave people alone. Many of us have a hidden belief (well, hidden from ourselves, often obvious to everyone else) that the world's functioning is all up to us. We have moved from a healthy sense of responsibility to a hypervigilant sense that the people under our responsibility should be under our control. We worry while they complete their responsibilities, as if we believe our worry will motivate them and carry them through, because we can't let go of that illusion of control.

When I was in high school and college, I sometimes cleaned houses as a part-time job. During one summer, I regularly cleaned for a wealthy woman who said she liked my thorough work but followed me around the house as if she thought I would steal, destroy or mutilate her most valuable possessions. She tried to be subtle about it, finding excuses to hover nearby, but she was actually maddeningly obvious. Every so often, she would jump in with a "suggestion" or observation. I was thrilled to walk away from that house for the last time, and not just because scrubbing someone else's toilet (or my own, for that matter) is not my favorite way to spend a day. I was not free to do my best, or most efficient, work with her worrying over whether I was doing it the way she would. I never could figure out why she didn't do it herself. She certainly didn't save any time or effort by hiring me.

Impaired judgment. Worry can cause us to make short-sighted decisions that fail us in the long term. It can also keep us from doing the right thing. We become so focused on the possible danger in a good choice that we enter a sort of "risk paralysis," lose courage and go for an easier, more comfortable option.

We decide not to share out of our abundance because we're worried we won't have enough for ourselves. We fail to extend hospitality because we worry that our houses aren't clean enough or people won't like our cooking or we might invite in someone dangerous. We refuse to commit to relationships because we're afraid someone better will come along. We fail to speak the truth—sometimes for decades— because we're worried that we'll spark a conflict or people we love might leave us.

Some women choose abortion because they're desperately worried about their ability to navigate a future with a child in it—and then may live with long-term emotional pain as a result. Men abandon their families before they even start because they're worried about losing their freedom or failing to provide. We keep our kids off the bus, locked up at home and completely away from the Internet because we're worried about what might happen to them—and in the process we undermine their long-term strength, discernment and other essential skills. We say no to the next challenge because we're worried we might fail.

Some of us hoard money we should be spending because we're worried we'll run out. Others of us spend money we don't have because we're worried the opportunities we face won't come around again. We worry about our careers and sacrifice our families. We worry about our families and neglect the gifts God has given us. We ignore the people God has made us to be because we need to save up a little more security. We squirrel away, avoid risks, keep our heads down until we get twenty or forty or sixty years down the road and realize we haven't lived the lives we wish we had—all because we were worried about things that never happened. In recent years, millions of people have discovered how far this approach gets you when the economy crumbles underneath your life savings.

In 2008, financial experts estimated that American workers had lost 20 percent of the value of their retirement savings, or two trillion

dollars.[21] This happened over the course of only fifteen months. For
workers who had placed their trust in the stock market and spent their
lives looking forward to "someday," this loss was crushing. For those
close to retirement, this was devastating—and cause for more worry.

How many of these people had ignored much of what God had
called them to and invested only in their financial future, only to
discover their houses were built on shifting sand? How many of them
now lie awake at night, still worried over the treasure that has suddenly vanished? Their plans and preparations came to nothing.
Choices driven by worry are not wise choices. They are motivated by
self-protection, self-soothing or an overreach for control. They almost
always mean we live more conservatively than we should or fail to
anticipate the consequences of a reckless act.

Recklessness isn't the only problem; sometimes worry provides a
way to engage with a problem but avoid doing something about it.
For example, many people worry about the direction their churches
are headed but fail to get involved in a way that exercises influence.
Most adults worry about young people who are growing up without
positive role models, but not many volunteer to serve as mentors.
Nearly everyone is worried about people who are poor, oppressed and
disenfranchised, but relatively few are willing to make the kind of
sacrifice required to make even a small difference. It's easy to get
onboard with an awareness campaign and to worry publically to
show you're involved and then walk away without actually doing
anything at all.

Finally, worry can keep us from recognizing and responding to the
Holy Spirit's direction. Again, it's a matter of focus. When we're
worried, we may not even realize how much of our attention is consumed by the treadmill running "at the back of our minds." My sister
Kate told me, "When I find myself worrying, I feel a sense of inner
turmoil. I'm uneasy, irritable and distracted."

With the ubiquity of mobile phones and other electronic devices, we hear a lot about distracted driving these days. Most states have passed laws related to driving while distracted—with the majority banning text messaging and many states outlawing the use of handheld cell phones while driving.[22] There's a reason our governments don't take this issue lightly. In 2009, 20 percent of vehicle crashes with injuries reportedly involved distracted driving. Text messaging while driving makes a person twenty-three times more likely to crash. Using a cell phone while driving causes a 37-percent reduction in the amount of brain power dedicated to driving. And it delays a driver's reaction time as much as driving with a blood-alcohol level of .08 percent, the highest legal limit in most places.[23]

With such serious potential for impairment, it's absolutely stupid to engage in such distraction, and yet many people do. One poll found that "most drivers who own cell phones use them while driving even though almost all of them believe it is dangerous to do so." According to this poll, 25 percent of drivers with cell phones text while driving. And even in states that have banned the use of hand-held cell phones while driving, half of drivers with cell phones use them anyway.[24]

When we use our phones while driving, we are inviting distraction. And sometimes we use our cell phones specifically because we want to be distracted. Worrying produces a similar result, with anxiety drawing our attention away from the signs and signals God puts in our path. Our own internal conversations keep us from engaging in the conversation God wants to have with us.

The Holy Spirit is a gift some of us take for granted. How amazing that the very Spirit of God lives in his people and calls our attention to a level of reality we would not otherwise discern. This Spirit will comfort us with assurance of God's presence, give us empathy for hurting people we might otherwise dislike, correct us when we wander and illuminate the truth of God's Word. How tragic that we allow the worries of this world to silence this inner voice that speaks to us. Perhaps he is calling us to a new task, a new perspective or an act of faith. Perhaps he wishes to point out someone who needs our help. The proper attitude toward the Holy Spirit is one of listening—purposeful spiritual stillness that allows us to hear his voice. Ironically, while we are wringing our hands and trying to figure out how we can help God intervene on our behalf, the Holy Spirit may be speaking words of comfort, or even resolution, we are too preoccupied to hear.

Dissatisfaction. Much of our worry is driven by efforts to keep up with the Joneses in pursuit of the American dream. Consider for a moment how your anxiety level would be affected if you didn't have a mortgage or monthly rental payment you had to stretch to reach, if you didn't own (or need) a car, if you weren't striving to earn enough to finance the lifestyle you want for your family, if you lived in a cave, surrounded by other cave-dwellers equally unfamiliar with Ikea, granite countertops and MBAs. You would still worry, for sure, but you would be missing a layer of worry-fuel that plagues prosperous and achievement-oriented people like us. In our aspirational culture, we are always reaching for the next big thing, constantly hearing marketing messages that tell us we need something we never would have felt the need for on our own. And we worry over these newly discovered "needs." We also worry that what we have achieved will be taken away, will grow irrelevant or won't be good enough. When I asked my friend Michele what worries her, she mentioned, "There is so much pressure to earn more money, have a better job and keep up with the Joneses. Without these pressures, life would be simpler."

This achievement culture extends beyond our quest for what we see in the mall and our neighbors' driveways. Many of us feel tremendous pressure to always make more of ourselves, constantly moving up that corporate ladder or whatever ladder we happen to be on. Good enough is never good enough, and each generation is expected to achieve greater educational and career success than the one before. In many families, this mindset develops early. My friend Cory, who has accomplished a great deal at a young age, talked about his struggle with worry as a student: "I was quite a nervous person, usually tied to grades, life plan and fear of not overachieving." Another friend, Deb, credited her family culture with stoking the fire of worry in her: "I always wanted to do my best to please my parents, and then to please others like a boss at work or family members." She was expected to perform at a certain level, and like many of us she developed an anxious drive to achieve some unnamed level of success. For many of us, this level always seems to be just beyond our reach.

Regardless of whether we're satisfied with our achievements, many of us are tremendously invested in making sure others perceive us as successful. We worry over whether we look good to people—physically, personally and professionally. We fuss over projecting the right image and then managing that image. We worry over what people will say about us privately and publically.

In this age of social networking and digital imagery, this concern is not just for those who technically live in the public eye. In a sense, we all do. Our images can be plastered anywhere. A hasty, thoughtless statement typed in the middle of the night can define us. Our virtual identities—detached from the personal nuances that often convince others to grant us grace—are preserved forever. And in a culture increasingly defined by false images of beauty and public personas projected by teams of paid staff, the average person can't compete. We are worried for a reason.

For Cory, a common source of worry is "what other people think of me. Am I doing 'enough' with my life, am I making a big enough impact for others to notice, and do people find me abnormal because of life choices or because I'm a single adult man?" Deb, too, worries "about what others think, how I'm perceived, whether people will value my work." This is a source of worry we don't like to admit and don't typically share with others. But we're all concerned about how others perceive us, and for some of us this worry is consuming. For some of us, this kind of worry motivates us to a life of trying to be someone we weren't made to be, someone who makes us desperately unhappy.

The irony about achieving what we want is that we bring ourselves to a whole new level of anxiety. In addition to our worries over what we're striving for, we start worrying about keeping what we have. This kind of worry may be focused on material possessions, circumstances that make us feel comfortable or safe, or people who are important to us.

I talked with one woman who echoed what I think many people would say: "The number-one thing I worry about is finances, and how they impact my security. My rational side has to remind my emotional side that money and the source of it come and go despite our best efforts." Regardless of how much we have, we want more. And the more we have, the more we have to lose. Even though the thought of losing what we have may keep us from enjoying it, we still worry over the possibility that it might someday be gone. (More on this in chapter 8.)

Exhaustion. As my friend Michele said, "Worry never changes anything." And as Corrie ten Boom, a famous survivor of a Nazi concentration camp, said, "Worry does not empty tomorrow of its sorrow, it empties today of its strength."

Worry wears us out. It's physically exhausting, as a friend of mine just learned. Two days ago, she visited her dentist in the morning and found out she needed a root canal, which was scheduled for late that afternoon. She spent the whole day worried about the procedure, feeling so anxious she couldn't be productive and had to take some time off work. After the root canal, she went home and relaxed and wondered what she had been so worried about. She had to rest though. She was surprised at how physically exhausted she was from her day of anxiety.

But the consequences aren't only physical. Worry wears us out emotionally and spiritually as well.

Several months ago, I was invited to a daylong consultation and brainstorming session at a company in the area. I have a chronic problem with running late, so naturally that morning I was worried that I would be late and make a bad impression. I was even more anxious about presenting myself well, being helpful and getting through the day without convincing anyone I'm an idiot. I spent too much time and energy trying to figure out what to wear, which meant I was running late as feared. Then as I was leaving, I remembered I had failed to tell my hosts I'm a vegetarian. I started worrying they wouldn't have any vegetarian-friendly lunch food. So I threw a few snacks in my purse, delaying my departure even more. Then I pondered over whether to bring a water bottle and finally decided they would have water there.

By the time I rushed out the door and jumped into my car, I was a frantic mess. I tore down the streets, going as fast as I dared. In my head, I screamed at the stoplights in front of me, begging them to stay or turn green. As I approached a set of train tracks where I'd been delayed before, I mentally yelled at all the trains which might be in the Chicago metropolitan area and begged them to stay away from this particular intersection until I was across. When I found myself mentally chanting, *No trains, no trains,* I suddenly realized how tense and anxious I was, irrationally trying to use mental telepathy to tell inanimate objects what to do.

Thinking it might help calm me, I turned on the radio. At that very moment someone was reading aloud from Luke 12:22-31: "Jesus said, 'That is why I tell you not to worry about everyday life—whether you have enough food to eat or enough clothes to wear. For life is more than food, and your body more than clothing. . . . Don't be concerned about what to eat and what to drink. Don't worry about such things. These things dominate the thoughts of unbelievers all over the world, but your Father already knows your needs. Seek the Kingdom of God above all else, and he will give you everything you need.'"

I had to laugh out loud. All morning I had been worrying, literally, about what to eat, drink and wear. I was trying to make decisions among the abundance God had already provided. In my focus on trivial matters, I had already exhausted myself before even leaving the house—and it hadn't helped me at all.

Our work lives are the focal point for much worry. Some of us worry over our work to the point where we can't seem to stop working, even when we're long past the point of true effectiveness. Partly due to the demands of an economic culture that values productivity over effectiveness, efficiency over engagement and outcome over process, many of us have lost our sense of rhythm and don't even recognize our need for breaks. Some have abandoned the idea of investing our gifts in anything besides work, because work either demands so much of us or numbs us with mundane responsibilities, so we don't expect to have anything left at the end of the day. Our worry drives us to keep pounding away at work until it's done or we run out of time. The concept of setting aside a grueling project so we can come back to it later feels about as useful, and acceptable, as falling asleep on the job. Yet evidence suggests intentional napping at work actually may be useful,[25] and so is walking away from work and engaging in something else.

We weren't made to work all the time. Yet many of us have so much to do, we really could work all the time and probably never run out of things to do. This reality burdens us and, of course, encourages us to worry. When we express our worry through work, we usually end up reaching a point of seriously diminishing returns, when we're accomplishing very little. Yet the thought of stopping seems out of the question, so we keep at it. And even when we do walk away, our minds often stay in the workplace, sorting and resorting through all that needs to be done.

On several occasions, I have worked late into the night only to discover the next day that my exhausted self had done such sloppy work, or made such errors in judgment, that I had to do the whole thing over. I've also worried over projects and problems so much that by the time I sat down to actually do something about them, I was paralyzed by my own thoughts and couldn't figure out where to begin. Like the "drinking bird" toys that remain fixated on a glass of water, constantly moving and sticking their beaks in the water but never drinking, I wasted my time and energy just because I was worried.

Spiritual myopia. Worry encourages a kind of spiritual nearsightedness, blurring our vision of God's work in the world. When we remain focused on what scares us, we may lose sight of the ways God blesses us, cares for us and the people we love, and sustains our world. We may even miss the ways he redeems the bad things that happen to us, bringing good from bad, beauty from pain, according to his purposes. Even when we are aware of God's good gifts, worry can keep us from enjoying them because we're waiting for something bad to happen or thinking about the unknown future.

When I was in ninth grade, I went to a large junior high school with big classrooms and teachers who wrote a lot of notes on the chalkboard (yes, actual chalk!). Up to that point, I had only been in tiny schools where much of the learning happened more individually, the rooms were small, and I rarely had to see something on the other side of the room. So I had no idea I had terrible vision. I thought it was normal to squint constantly, experience pounding headaches at the end of the day and see (or not see) things the way I did.

When my new teachers realized I couldn't see the board, even from the front row, they recommended an eye exam. I had had plenty of eye exams before, but I had always squinted my way through the eye charts and had been told my eyes were *almost* bad enough to need glasses, but not quite. So I expected the same result. But this eye doctor noticed my squinting and told me I wasn't allowed to do that during the test. "Then how am I supposed to see the letters?" I asked. It turned out I couldn't legitimately see any of them—even the enormous *E* at the top of the chart. I was legally blind.

When I put on my first pair of glasses about a week later, I was overcome by a sensation of relaxation spreading through my whole head, to the point where I felt like I was going to fall asleep. My eyes—which had been terribly strained—started to water as they released their tension and settled into looking through the new lenses. I looked out the window of the eyeglasses store at the fast-food restaurants across the street, and I couldn't believe I could read their signs. I walked outside and looked at the ground and was astonished to realize I could differentiate individual blades of grass. I could see leaves on the trees, grains of dirt. I had thought my vision was normal, and I'd had no idea I was *supposed* to be able to see details. All I ever saw, from more than a few feet away, was blocks of color and blobs of light.

Worry gives our spirits the same sort of myopia. As long as we're focused on the worries we hold in front of us, we miss the real story of God's good work all around us. Like my vision, this kind of near-sightedness is fully correctable with the right lenses. We must let go of worry and look through trust.

When we worry instead, we hold on to the idea that we must maintain control over things that are not ours. That we can't stop thinking about what concerns us and the best use of our faculties is treading over worn ground just for the sake of staying there. That there must be something we can and should do about every situation that grabs our awareness. We elevate ourselves and our own responsibilities above God's. We diminish our own view of God's capabilities. We also assume the people around us can't be trusted.

As my friend Cory said, "Worry has hurt me by causing me to question and not fully trust people and the Lord." We were created to have trusting relationships with God and other people. On this warped planet, plenty comes between us and those we should trust—worry is just one of many problems. But its effect is significant, keeping us closed and emotionally stingy, carrying burdens we don't have to carry.

I love football. One of the reasons I enjoy watching it is because success is so dependent on team dynamics. For a football team to run successful plays—and win games—all eleven players on the field must trust their coaches and each other. If eleven people try to run eleven different plays at the same time, the results will be disastrous. They have to let the coaches or the quarterback tell them which plays to run. In any given play, no two people on the field have the same assignment. No one is expendable. And if one person blows his assignment, the whole team suffers. If one player decides to do another player's job for him—for example, if the right guard doesn't trust the tackle positioned next to him, he may sacrifice his assignment to make up for the tackle's deficiency, putting the running back at risk—the team will never make it downfield. Individual players don't always know whether others are living up to what's been asked of them. They have to do their part to the best of their ability and hope others are doing the same. The people who see the big picture and know where the plays are breaking down are the coaches. When players listen to their coaches, understand what they've been asked to do and do it well, they can expect some success.

Essentially, all worry comes down to a matter of trust—not a cheap, episodic trust, but a deep undercurrent of faith-fueled confidence informed by belief in the nature of God as he has revealed himself. God asks us to trust him, and he presents such trust as the antithesis of worry. For those of us who instead trust in people, material possessions, and "chariots and horses" (Ps 20:7), worry is only natural. The objects of our trust will fail at some point—probably at multiple points—and will ultimately prove just as limited as we are, perhaps even more so.

When we fail to trust God, we behave like frantic sheep who have forgotten they're following a shepherd. Sheep are made to follow one leader. If that leader is a good shepherd, they will have all they need. They will find rest in green pastures and beside peaceful streams. They will always find their way home. Even when they walk through un-imaginably dark valleys, their shepherd will stay close beside them. They will know this about the shepherd: "Your rod and your staff protect and comfort me" (Ps 23:4).

A flock of sheep that stopped trusting their shepherd and decided to go it alone, instead trusting only in themselves and their fellow sheep, would find themselves wandering aimlessly in panicked circles. When danger arrived, they would be frantic with misdirected running, trying to get away from the threat but not knowing where to go. And if they trusted the voices of those who would gladly prey on them—like foxes, wolves and bears—they would find themselves being a quick dinner. How ridiculous it would be for sheep to behave this way with their shepherd standing among them, calling to them and showing them the way to go.

Of course, this is exactly the metaphor used in Matthew 9:36, de-scribing Jesus' response when he saw the crowds of people who came to see him seeking healing and truth: "He had compassion on them because they were confused and helpless, like sheep without a shepherd." The Good News Bible translation says, "They were worried and helpless, like sheep without a shepherd."

God does not condemn us for the many ways we worry any more than he condemns us for the other self-destructive choices we make, which are covered by Jesus' sacrifice on the cross. But he has created a world in which we suffer the consequences of these choices, and God does grieve over our unnecessary pain. And he does covet the attention we give to worry at the expense of his mission for us. God is calling all of us to step out and be different from our worried world, exercising such determined trust in him that we actually let go of worry.

We can always, always trust God. He is the only one who sees the big picture. We can't always trust other people, but sometimes we must take the risk. Worry keeps us trusting in ourselves (or no one) instead.

A Better Way: Sabbath

Worry also weighs on our bodies and spirits, even as our worries propel us into ever more frantic efforts to regain control. The biblical remedy for worry and exhaustion was the opposite of frantic effort, and God still calls us to this counterintuitive lifestyle. He calls us to sabbath rest—trust in God's provision. Sabbath is the ancient ritual practice of rest days God established among his people in the Old Testament. God first modeled this concept at the creation of the world, when he stopped creating and "rested from all his work." At that time, "God blessed the seventh day and declared it holy," set apart for some special and sacred purpose (Gen 2:2-3).

There is no more mention of this seventh day, or the concept of sabbath, in Scripture until Exodus 16, when the ancestors of Abraham, Isaac and Jacob were traveling from slavery in Egypt to destiny and purpose as God's people in the land he had promised them. On their way through the wilderness, before they reached Mt. Sinai and received the third commandment (along with the other nine), God introduced the practice of sabbath.

When the people were hungry, they received the food they needed in the form of manna, a supernatural provision that blanketed the ground each morning. God instructed them to gather food each day, and he introduced a curious discipline into the process: they were to gather only enough for that one day. For seriously hungry people traveling through a wilderness in ancient times, this was one tough act of faith. And God meant this to test their faith: "Each day the people can go out and pick up as much food as they need for that day. I will test them in this to see whether or not they will follow my instructions" (Ex 16:4). They had to trust that God would provide what they needed the next day too.

With the exception of the sixth day—the day before the sabbath—they were not allowed to prepare for their survival beyond the day they had been given. On the very first sabbath day, the people were surprised when no manna appeared, even though they had been told this would happen:

> Some of the people went out anyway on the seventh day, but they found no food. The LORD asked Moses, "How long will these people refuse to obey my commands and instructions? They must realize that the Sabbath is the LORD's gift to you. That is why he gives you a two-day supply on the sixth day, so there will be enough for two days. On the Sabbath day you must each stay in your place. Do not go out to pick up food on the seventh day." (Ex 16:27-29)

On that seventh day, the sabbath, God asked his people to exercise their faith by resting, trusting that what he had provided for them would sustain them, that he owned everything they needed, that there would be more tomorrow and that he was worthy of their trust. On the other six days of the week, he asked them to exercise their faith by gathering only enough for that day (plus enough for one more day on the sixth day). All week—not only on the seventh day—he asked them to rest in him.

The observance of sabbath is reaffirmed in Exodus 20, when these same people stood before a mountain called Sinai, where God revealed his Ten Commandments. The people of Israel were commanded to "remember to observe the Sabbath day by keeping it holy" (Ex 20:8). The requirement was clarified: they were to make the seventh day "a Sabbath day of rest dedicated to the LORD your God. On that day no one in your household may do any work" (Ex 20:10).

Thus began a ritual rhythm of rest days for God's people, a weekly occasion to stop working—at God's command—and to trust in God's provision. Under the covenant God made with his chosen nation, this weekly observance was critical to remaining faithful to the covenant. And for observant Jews, it remains sacred to this day.

Throughout their journey to the Promised Land, God's people

questioned his provision, rejected his gifts and doubted his goodness. Finally, they forfeited the Promised Land itself when they doubted God's ability to give it to them. God withheld the provision, the sabbath rest he had offered them:

> And who was it who rebelled against God, even though they heard his voice? Wasn't it the people Moses led out of Egypt? And who made God angry for forty years? Wasn't it the people who sinned, whose corpses lay in the wilderness? And to whom was God speaking when he took an oath that they would never enter his rest? Wasn't it the people who disobeyed him? So we see that because of their unbelief they were not able to enter his rest. (Heb 3:16-19)

But this ritual of rest was not the true and ultimate sabbath. Like the sacrificial system and the law itself, the weekly sabbath observance was a foreshadowing of what would come in God's new covenant with his people. The sabbath was fulfilled in Jesus' death and resurrection, when he made complete provision of all we need for forgiveness and righteousness before God. He made it possible for all those who trust in him to rest permanently from the requirements of sacrifice. To rest from striving to attain salvation from sin by keeping the law. No need for further spiritual toil to satisfy the requirements of his holiness. "So there is a special rest still waiting for the people of God. For all who have entered into God's rest have rested from their labors, just as God did after creating the world. So let us do our best to enter that rest" (Heb 4:9-11). This is the true rest, and all Christians have entered into this permanent state of spiritual rest. But many of us don't realize it.

The opposite of exhaustion, sabbath rest is ultimately trust in the sufficiency of Christ's sacrifice on our behalf. It's also a lifestyle that rests from efforts to provide for ourselves what God has already provided, a life built on faith that he will give us all we need. It means resting from our efforts to make our own way toward heaven, to control what has not been given to us to control, to make provision for what he has not provided, to make ourselves lovable or valuable through what we do.

This kind of sabbath is not encapsulated in a weekly observance; it's a permanent spiritual condition to enjoy. When we dwell in worry instead, we reject God's rest just as his ancient people did. We opt, instead, for spiritual exhaustion. Our rest, through Jesus, is for every day and every aspect of our lives. Worry is a special kind of toil that attempts to wrest control from God, to provide for ourselves, to store up for the future. Sabbath rest, on the other hand, is acknowledging our own limitations and leaving provision in God's hands.

When Jesus used that analogy about sheep without a shepherd, he was traveling throughout the region around the Sea of Galilee. He created a stir by preaching and healing people he met. Vast numbers came to see him, and he was moved by their aimless desperation. Read that description again: "They were confused and helpless, like sheep without a shepherd" (Mt 9:36). What an apt description of our culture! May we place our trust in him and instead conform to these words: "My sheep listen to my voice; I know them, and they follow me" (Jn 10:27).

We are not sheep without a shepherd. For people who claim to trust in God, worry is unnecessary, hypocritical and insulting to him. As one friend told me, "Worrying for me boils down to not holding on to that fact that God is the all-powerful, all-knowing and ever-loving Father. I often have to remind myself that he knows when a bird falls from its nest and that he clothes the flowers in the field."

Besides observing a regular rhythm of sabbath days, here are a few ideas for expressing a permanent state of spiritual sabbath rest in your life.

First of all, if you truly are responsible to do something, and you're worrying about it instead, do it! No amount of rest and relaxation or spiritual assurance will make up for the fact that you're dodging your responsibility. Once you have taken action, you won't have any more reason to worry about it.

On an ongoing basis, take care of yourself. Exercise, eat well, establish healthy sleep habits, take time to rest, spend time with people you love, take a break from worry to do something you enjoy and refresh your perspective. Chances are, when your break is over, your worries won't look so attractive. Occasionally, try taking a break to just be still. We often express worry through constant movement. Set a timer for five or ten minutes, sit or lie still and read Psalm 46.

Change your focus. Take some advice from Philippians 4:8 and "fix your thoughts on what is true, and honorable, and right, and pure, and lovely, and admirable."

Take some time to enjoy the way God has made you. Express yourself! Are you artistic? Create something beautiful. Precise? Complete a puzzle. Handy? Fix the leaky faucet. Helpful? Serve someone else. Do something that channels your energy toward where you "feel God's pleasure," in the words of Eric Liddell of *Chariots of Fire* fame. Use the gifts God has given you, and delight in them.

It's okay to enjoy life! When God gives you joy, indulge it. When your circumstances or your spirit fill with happiness, go ahead and be happy—even if you know it won't last. These moments are gifts from God. Give yourself permission to stop thinking about bad things and enjoy good things. After all, "a cheerful heart is good medicine, but a broken spirit saps a person's strength" (Prov 17:22). This is more than just a well-worn biblical saying—it's scientifically proven!

If we claim to place our trust in the only all-powerful, all-knowing, all-wise being in existence, who is full of grace and love, unlimited in every way—and yet still feel the need to worry, we need to revisit our view of God. We need to grow in trust. That doesn't mean pretending bad things don't happen in this life—it means trusting him so much we can live at peace despite the dangers, horrors and grief we face, knowing he and his plans are greater than all of them. Knowing death is always at our heels but is a defeated enemy. And God is calling all of us to just that kind of growth.

4

What God Says About Worry

Our worry offends God for at least two reasons—because it reflects our anemic view of him and because it destroys people, whom he loves beyond measure, and dramatically limits our potential for life as he wants us to live it. Like all rebellion against God, worry impairs our relationship with him. But don't take my word for it. Let's consider what God's Word says on the subject.

Many people are familiar with a few key Bible passages that specifically mention worry. I already mentioned one such passage in chapter three: Luke 12:22-31. Philippians 4:6-7 is another: "Don't worry about anything; instead, pray about everything. Tell God what you need, and thank him for all he has done. Then you will experience God's peace, which exceeds anything we can understand. His peace will guard your hearts and minds as you live in Christ Jesus."

These are powerful and instructive verses, but we shouldn't limit our exploration to these two passages. God's Word has so much more to say about worry. In fact, a look through the Bible reveals worry is a big problem and a high priority in God's relationship with people. This makes sense, since God also highly prioritizes faith—the one thing he asks from us in return for his lavish grace. Hebrews 11 makes clear—through the examples of weak, confused and inadequate people of faith—that what really matters most to God is our faith, our trusting response to him. We often think that in "Bible times" people found it easier to follow God than we do now. But in the stories recorded in the Bible, God asked people for faith in very difficult circumstances, in some ways much harder than our own.

Consider the following sampling of passages that address worry, directly or indirectly. Note that some of these passages speak of "fear," but I believe the references to fear in these verses are addressing something akin to worry, rather than the automatic fear response I discussed in chapter one. Worry often means choosing to stay in a place of fear—an ongoing condition of fear when we could make another choice. God is asking his people to choose to believe and trust in him, even though they usually have good reasons to worry and they may still feel fear as a sensation that helps them respond to a real threat. In several cases, this sense of worry, or choosing to stay afraid, is suggested by the context. In other places, it's suggested in the original language.

OLD TESTAMENT ASSURANCE

In Genesis 15, we read about Abram several years after God called him to leave Ur and go to an unknown place, announced he would make Abram's name great, and promised to give him many descendants. Abram finds himself living as a stranger in that new land (Canaan) and still without a single descendant. His wife, Sarai, hasn't yet suggested he produce a descendant with her servant Hagar, and Abram doubts God's promises to him. In a vision, God told him, "Do not be afraid, Abram, for I will protect you, and your reward will be great."

Abram's questions in this passage suggest more than simple fear, the kind we would associate with a real and imminent threat. They suggest worried speculation over whether he should continue living by faith: "O Sovereign LORD, what good are all your blessings when I don't even have a son?" (v. 2). "O Sovereign LORD, how can I be sure that I will actually possess [the land of Canaan]?" (v. 8). God responds with a powerful illustration of the covenant between him and Abram. He tells Abram to let go of his fear, and when Abraham, living by a new name, chooses to believe God's promises, God demonstrates how much he values our faith in him: "The Lord counted him as righteous because of his faith" (v. 6).

When we catch up with Abraham's son Isaac, in Genesis 26, God has blessed Isaac with wealth, as he had Isaac's father. This great wealth (in the form of large flocks and herds of animals) make the locals (the Philistines) nervous, so they fill Isaac's wells with dirt and ask Isaac to move on—and he does. But everywhere he goes with his family and servants and animals, the Philistines don't want him around, so he keeps moving. When he finally finds a spot to settle, at Beersheba, God appears to him and repeats the promise he had made to Abraham: to give Isaac many descendants and make them into a great nation. But first he addresses Isaac's fear, which probably has increased as he worried over finding a place for his household in the land of Canaan: "Do not be afraid, for I am with you and will bless you" (v. 24).

As God had promised, Abraham did have many descendants, and they did become a great nation. God had also promised Abraham that his descendants would be in a foreign land for four hundred years and would be enslaved—and sure enough, they lived as strangers in a land they didn't own, and eventually they were enslaved in Egypt. In Exodus 14, soon after God liberates them from Egypt, they find themselves seemingly trapped between Pharaoh's army and the Red Sea. The people panic and ask Moses,

Why did you bring us out here to die in the wilderness? Weren't there enough graves for us in Egypt? What have you done to us? Why did you make us leave Egypt? Didn't we tell you this would happen while we were still in Egypt? We said, "Leave us alone! Let us be slaves to the Egyptians. It's better to be a slave in Egypt than a corpse in the wilderness!" (vv. 11-12)

Moses' response? "Don't be afraid. Just stand still and watch the LORD rescue you today. The Egyptians you see today will never be seen again. The LORD himself will fight for you. Just stay calm" (vv. 13-14).

And that's exactly what happens. When Abraham's descendants take a few steps of faith, God parts the waters of the Red Sea and allows them to cross before the waters rush back over the doomed Egyptian chariots and their riders.

Later, before a new generation of Israelites enters the land God has promised to them, Moses takes the opportunity to address them three times, reminding them of who they are, how they are to live, what God has done for them and what he has promised. Moses' three sermons make up nearly the entire book of Deuteronomy, and throughout he reminds his listeners how much God values their trust in him and their courageous steps of faith.

He recalls what he told the people—this crowd's parents and grandparents—when they first reached the land of Canaan: "Look! He has placed the land in front of you. Go and occupy it as the LORD, the God of your ancestors, has promised you. Don't be afraid! Don't be discouraged!" (Deut 1:21). He repeats what he told Joshua about the coming entry into the Promised Land: "Do not be afraid of the nations there, for the LORD your God will fight for you" (Deut 3:22).

He reminds this new generation that the people whose lands they will conquer are stronger than them. But then he encourages them, "But don't be afraid of them! Just remember what the LORD your God did to Pharaoh and to all the land of Egypt" (Deut 7:18). Then he repeats his encouragement: "No, do not be afraid of those nations, for the LORD your God is among you, and he is a great and awesome God"

(Deut 7:21). The word used here is *'arats,* which means "to tremble, dread, fear, oppress, prevail, break, be terrified, cause to tremble."[1] This sounds like a worried sort of "afraid" to me—dwelling in a state of fear.

Later, Moses again calls the people to abandon worry and fear and replace them with trust in the Lord: "When you go out to fight your enemies and you face horses and chariots and an army greater than your own, do not be afraid. The LORD your God, who brought you out of the land of Egypt, is with you!" He tells them the priest must speak to the troops before battle. "He will say to them, 'Listen to me, all you men of Israel! Do not be afraid as you go out to fight your enemies today! Do not lose heart or panic or tremble before them'" (Deut 20:1-3).

And finally, Moses wraps up his final sermon with more of the same advice in Deuteronomy 31:6-8: "So be strong and courageous! Do not be afraid and do not panic before them. For the LORD your God will personally go ahead of you. He will neither fail you nor abandon you. . . . Do not be afraid or discouraged, for the LORD will personally go ahead of you. He will be with you; he will neither fail you nor abandon you."

He never tells the people to stop worrying because there is nothing to worry about—he acknowledges they have reasons to be afraid! But they are supposed to reject fear, worry and panic because God is with them, will fight for them and will not abandon them.

Later, after Moses' death, God speaks to Joshua, the new leader of the Israelites. In the space of eleven sentences (and three verses in our Bibles) in Joshua 1, God tells Joshua three times, "Be strong and courageous!" He also tells him to reject worry and dismay—again, not simply for the sake of putting on a good show for the people, but because God is with him: "This is my command—be strong and courageous! Do not be afraid or discouraged. For the LORD your God is with you wherever you go" (Josh 1:9).

Later, in Joshua 8, as the Israelites are conquering the land of Canaan, they are shocked, in light of God's promises, to lose a battle (and some of their fighters) to the army of Ai. God reveals to Joshua that they have lost the fight because someone has broken the rules and kept some plunder for himself. Once the lawbreaker (Achan) is discovered and punished, God tells Joshua to attack Ai again. After the defeat, which had left the leaders of Israel terrified and grieving, Joshua must have been very worried about their chances in a second battle. But God tells him not to worry: "Then the LORD said to Joshua, 'Do not be afraid or discouraged. Take all your fighting men and attack Ai, for I have given you the king of Ai, his people, his town, and his land'" (Josh 8:1).

Generations later, in Elisha's time, 2 Kings 6 tells us Israel was at war with the Arameans. God gives Elisha the ability to discern the plans of the king of Aram, and he warns the king of Israel, so they repeatedly avoid the Arameans' attack. The king of Aram becomes aware that Elisha is foiling his plans, and he sends out an army to surround the city where Elisha is and capture him.

When Elisha's servant gets up early the next morning and sees soldiers, horses and chariots surrounding the city, he is understandably worried. But Elisha gives him another perspective: "'Don't be afraid!' Elisha tells him. 'For there are more on our side than on theirs!'" (2 Kings 6:16). Elisha prays that the servant will be able to see the full spiritual reality of the situation, and he does: "He saw that the hillside around Elisha was filled with horses and chariots of fire" (6:17). Again, Elisha has a very good reason to calm his servant's nerves—he doesn't tell him to buck up or stop being so wimpy; he tells him to stop being afraid because God is literally and tangibly with them.

As the history of God's people marches forward, similar assurances continue. In 1 Chronicles 28:20, David encourages his son Solomon to build the temple: "Be strong and courageous, and do the work. Don't be afraid or discouraged, for the LORD God, my God, is with you."

In 2 Chronicles 20, facing foreign armies united against them, the people of Judah know they are outmatched. God's Spirit speaks through a man named Jahaziel and tells them, "Do not be afraid or discouraged. Go out against them tomorrow, for the LORD is with you!" (v. 17).

And in 2 Chronicles 32, God's people face another military threat when the brutal Assyrian army threatens to attack Jerusalem. King Hezekiah makes wise preparations and encourages the people: "Be strong and courageous! Don't be afraid or discouraged because of the king of Assyria or his mighty army, for there is a power far greater on our side!" (v. 7).

Many years later, the same assurance encourages the people of Judah who return from exile to repair and rebuild the wall of Jerusalem. They are threatened by enemies who don't like what they are doing and plan to attack them. Nehemiah, like Hezekiah, takes precautions and makes preparations to guard the workers. Nehemiah 4 tells us he then calls the people together and tells them, "Don't be afraid of the enemy! Remember the Lord, who is great and glorious, and fight for your brothers, your sons, your daughters, your wives, and your homes!" (v. 14).

The book of Psalms is full of encouragement to reject fear and worry and to trust in God instead. In Psalm 23, David writes about the security we can have when we trust in God as our shepherd, even when we walk through the darkest of valleys: "I will not be afraid, for you are close beside me. Your rod and your staff protect and comfort me" (v. 4).

In the beautiful and well-known Psalm 27, David again affirmed his confidence in God and asked, "The LORD is my light and my salvation—so why should I be afraid? The LORD is my fortress, protecting me from danger, so why should I tremble?"

The popular Psalm 46 is a powerful affirmation of trust in God. "Be still, and know that I am God!" verse 10 proclaims. The word translated "be still" in this verse is *raphah*, which can also be translated "relax" or "let go."[2]

In Psalm 56, David reflects on his experience when captured by Philistines—a legitimate cause for fear—and puts things in perspective: "I trust in God, so why should I be afraid? What can mere mortals do to me?" (v. 4).

In Psalm 62:5-8, again David affirms that his hope, help and strength come from God alone, even when he is surrounded by enemies. He admonishes, "O my people, trust in him at all times. Pour out your heart to him, for God is our refuge."

And in Psalm 118, the psalmist again writes the refrain of trust and proper perspective: "The LORD is for me, so I will have no fear. What can mere people do to me?" (v. 6).

Among the wisdom in the book of Proverbs is the idea that "fearing people is a dangerous trap, but trusting the LORD means safety" (Prov 29:25). The word translated "fearing," *charadah*, presented in contrast to trust, also means anxiety, trembling and anxious care.[3]

The prophet Isaiah has a lot to say about trust. His prophetic ministry began with a vision of God's overpowering glory, and this experience must have boosted Isaiah's confidence in the God he served. At the Spirit's direction, he proclaims many messages designed to inspire God's people to trust, based in a sense of awe at God's greatness.

When Syria and Israel team up for an attack on Judah, King Ahaz of Judah is understandably fearful. "The hearts of the king and his people trembled with fear, like trees shaking in a storm" (Is 7:2). God sends Isaiah to deliver a message to the king: "Tell him to stop worrying. Tell him he doesn't need to fear the fierce anger of those two burned-out embers, King Rezin of Syria and Pekah son of Remaliah" (7:4). Then he asks for the king's trust: "Unless your faith is firm, I cannot make you stand firm" (7:9).

Again in Isaiah 41, God asks his people to trust him in the context of a prophecy about future events. Three times in this chapter, he tells them, "Don't be afraid." But these aren't empty requests; each time, he gives them a reason to abandon their fear: "For I am with you." "I am here to help you." "I will help you." He doesn't tell them not to be afraid or discouraged because of who they are, because of their own strength or through an independent act of will. He tells them not to be afraid because of who he is.

NEW TESTAMENT REASSURANCE

God's instructions to choose faith instead of worry do not end with the closing of the Old Testament. Matthew 6, which records Jesus' famous Sermon on the Mount, contains one of the most well-known passages about worry. Jesus tells his listeners not to worry but to focus on God's priorities and trust God to provide what they need: "So don't worry about tomorrow, for tomorrow will bring its own worries. Today's trouble is enough for today" (v. 34).

Later Jesus commissions his twelve disciples for ministry in his name, giving them several instructions in the process. Four times in Matthew 10, he tells them not to worry or be afraid, and each time he explains why: God will give them the words to say when arrested; God is far more powerful than people, who can at worst merely kill the body; someday God will reveal everything that people try to hide; and God cares for even the smallest sparrow and loves people far more.

During his final Passover celebration with his disciples, often called the Last Supper, Jesus takes the opportunity to do some final teaching and to tell his closest followers about some things they should expect in the future. On this important occasion, as recorded in John 14, he twice tells them not to be troubled. The word translated "troubled" is *tarasso*, which can also be translated "anxious or distressed." This same word is used in 1 Peter 3:14 and translated as "worry."[4]

In John 14:1, Jesus contrasts troubled hearts with trust in God. In verse 27, he contrasts trouble with the peace that only God can give: "I am leaving you with a gift—peace of mind and heart. And the peace

I give is a gift the world cannot give. So don't be troubled or afraid."

The apostle Paul carries this theme through his writing. In his letter to the church in Rome, Paul makes clear that God does not want us to live in a state of fear, worried about God's punishment or anger (Rom 8). Instead, we should consider ourselves God's adopted children, dearly loved and permanently part of the family.

Paul closes his letter to the church at Philippi with some words of encouragement. As Jesus does in John 14, Paul contrasts agitation with God's peace. He instructs Christians, "Don't worry about anything; instead, pray about everything. . . . Then you will experience God's peace, which exceeds anything we can understand" (Phil 4:6-7).

Paul also writes about this same kind of peace in his letter to the church in Colossae. Among his instructions for living the Christian life, he tells them, "Let the peace that comes from Christ rule in your hearts. For as members of one body you are called to live in peace" (Col 3:15).

In his second letter to his protégé Timothy, Paul echoes his earlier letter to the Roman church, writing that we are not to be fearful and timid people (2 Tim 1:7).

In Hebrews 13, the author quotes two previous worry-related passages: Deuteronomy 31:6, 8 and Psalm 118:6. In doing so, this writer uses these two assurances from God to explain why we should not be greedy but should be satisfied with what we have. People who are content have far fewer reasons to worry.

So we can say with confidence,
"The LORD is my helper,
so I will have no fear.
What can mere people do to me?" (Heb 13:6)

In the first letter attributed to the apostle Peter, he gives a series of instructions for the way Christians should live and suggests that godly living will make his readers less likely to suffer persecution. Then he tells them not to worry or be afraid because "even if you suffer for doing what is right, God will reward you for it" (1 Pet 3:14). Later in the same letter, Peter instructs these suffering Christians to "give all your worries and cares to God, for he cares about you" (1 Pet 5:7).

Strong Words About Worry

In all these examples, we see how God reassured people, reminding them of his presence and asking for their faith-filled and trusting response. He recognized and addressed their fears, giving them reasons (such as "I am with you") not to worry. The Bible is filled with such examples.

On the other hand, the Bible also shows plenty of examples of people who felt God's displeasure because they worried rather than trusted him. The difference: in these passages, God and his prophet are not speaking to frightened people who need assurance of his presence with them; instead, these people had been given a clear chance to display their faith in the Lord—some of them numerous chances. God holds them accountable for what he has given them and for the response they have chosen: to worry. These stories should sober those of us who have free access to the biblical record, can feed at will on a rich diet of redemption stories and have seen God demonstrate his faithfulness in our own lives. We are accountable for whether we respond to these gifts with faith and trust in God.

Just a month into their trip from Egypt to the Promised Land, recorded in Exodus 16, the people of Israel are tested again, this time by hunger. Again they lose sight of what God has promised them and worry they will die from hunger. They complain anxiously, "'If only the Lord had killed us back in Egypt,' they moaned. 'There we sat around pots filled with meat and ate all the bread we wanted. But now you have brought us into this wilderness to starve us all to death'" (v. 3). They were actually pining for the days of slavery, rejecting God's gift of might and miraculous rescue and the promise of a future filled with purpose.

God tells Moses, "I will test them in this to see whether or not they will follow my instructions" (v. 4). And indeed, he devises a serious test of faith for hungry people. He instructs Moses to tell the people that God will provide all the food they need, and each day they can gather only enough for that day. On the sixth day of the week, they will receive enough for two days so they can rest on the seventh day. Some people decide to gather extra and save some for the next day—and their food rots. Others decide to gather on the seventh day—and find nothing.

God asks, "How long will these people refuse to obey my commands and instructions?" He is training his people to trust him, and their anxious refusal to obey reveals their desire to trust in themselves instead.

When the Israelites finally reached the land God has promised to give them, the land of Canaan, God tells Moses to send twelve men (one from each tribe) to explore the land and report back (Num 13). When they return, they bring reports of a fertile land, well settled with fortified cities and strong people. Ten of the scouts tell the people there is no way their ragtag band can conquer the people of Canaan. The remaining two, Caleb and Joshua, disagree—not because they believe the Israelites are stronger but because they believe God's promise: "They are only helpless prey to us! They have no protection, but the LORD is with us!" (Num 14:9).

But the people had already responded to the situation in panicked worry:

> Then the whole community began weeping aloud, and they cried all night. Their voices rose in a great chorus of protest against Moses and Aaron. "If only we had died in Egypt, or even here in the wilderness!" they complained. "Why is the LORD taking us to this country only to have us die in battle? Our wives and our little ones will be carried off as plunder! Wouldn't it be better

for us to return to Egypt?" Then they plotted among themselves,
"Let's choose a new leader and go back to Egypt!" (Num 14:1-4)

And even after they hear from Joshua and Caleb, the people refuse to
be convinced, refuse to trust God, refuse to claim the land God had
promised to give them. Again they long for the days of slavery, rejecting the freedom God had given them.

As a consequence for their worried lack of trust, despite the obvious ways God has shown his power and his care for them, none of
the people of that generation get to enter the Promised Land—except
Joshua and Caleb—because they don't live and think as God's people.

The people of Israel finally do take residence in the land of Canaan,
and generations later, during the time when judges rule them, they reject
God again. Tired of living in a theocracy, the people ask the prophet
Samuel to appoint a king over them. "We want to be like the nations
around us. Our king will judge us and lead us into battle," they say.

Samuel is unhappy with this request and takes it before God. "'Do
everything they say to you,' the LORD replied, 'for it is me they are
rejecting, not you. They don't want me to be their king any longer.
Ever since I brought them from Egypt they have continually abandoned me and followed other gods. And now they are giving you the
same treatment. Do as they ask, but solemnly warn them about the
way a king will reign over them'" (1 Sam 8:7-9).

A few chapters later, in 1 Samuel 12, Samuel crowns King Saul and
then makes clear that God is displeased with their request for a king.
He also suggests their request was motivated by fear of the brutal king
of the Ammonites: "But when you were afraid of Nahash, the king of
Ammon, you came to me and said that you wanted a king to reign
over you, even though the LORD your God was already your king" (1
Sam 12:12). Their worry leads them to seek a human leader and reject
the intimacy of God's direct leadership. And they suffer grief—over
and over—as a result.

During the time of Isaiah's ministry, when Judah faces a threat from the infamous Assyrian army, they again reject God. Rather than trust in God for help and obey his instructions, they give in to fear and worry and go to Egypt for help. The prophet Isaiah delivers God's message in response, recorded in Isaiah 30. He warns them that their alliance with Egypt will not turn out as they hope. He also affirms, later in the chapter, that those who trust in God will be blessed and cared for.

Jesus also has words of warning for those who reject God's gifts in favor of worry. In what's commonly called the parable of the talents, recorded in Matthew 25, Jesus uses a negative example of a servant who lets worry motivate him to act as a poor steward of what his master has given him. Afraid he will lose the money or earn additional money and be held accountable for more, he buries it in the ground rather than investing it or putting it to work.

When Jesus and his disciples are crossing the Sea of Galilee in a boat, they are caught in a severe storm and water starts filling the boat (Mk 4). The disciples are afraid and can't believe Jesus is sleeping through the whole thing. When they wake him and ask, "Teacher, don't you care that we're going to drown?" Jesus "rebuked the wind and . . . the waves" and then rebuked his disciples: "Why are you afraid? Do you still have no faith?" (vv. 38-40). Ironically, Jesus' calming of the storm makes them even more afraid.

When Jesus visits his friends Mary and Martha, in Luke 10, Martha is caught up in preparing a big meal and fumes at her sister, Mary, for hanging out with Jesus rather than helping her. When she asks Jesus to intervene, he must shock her when he rebukes her for worrying over the details of dinner rather than following her sister's example.

This list of Scriptures represents a lot of Bible passages—including some that are very familiar to many of us, but which we may not have looked at through the lens of what they say about worry. Clearly, God wants us to trust him. And clearly, he sees our worry—and our choice to stay in a place of fear—as betraying a lack of trust. God doesn't say, "Don't worry too much" or "Worry only about what really matters." He says, "Do not worry." "Do not fear." "Do not be afraid/troubled/anxious." He calls us to trust him, to acknowledge who he is and to live as if we are in a world he owns completely.

ADDRESSING WORRY WITH GOD'S WORD

It can be tempting to read a book like this one and nod along with the recitation of Bible passages, learn from what you read and move on to the next book. But books like this one—which most decidedly is not divinely inspired—are no substitute for the actual book containing God's very words and wisdom. Read it for yourself. Study some of the passages I've highlighted in this chapter. And if you're looking for some inspiration to help you break the habit of worry, you can start with the inspiring Scriptures I've included in appendix B. The way to change our habits of the heart and mind is to be transformed, and we cannot create soul-deep transformation in ourselves. That comes from God himself, and he often uses the tool of his Word. The Bible really is no ordinary book. If you invest in understanding it, it will change you. "For the word of God is alive and powerful. It is sharper than the sharpest two-edged sword, cutting between soul and spirit, between joint and marrow. It exposes our innermost thoughts and desires" (Heb 4:12).

As you read Scriptures that encourage you to trust God, try using those verses to practice trust. This might happen in baby steps. Practicing trust can be extremely difficult, especially for people who have been wounded or have suffered trauma and are worried about future trauma or about the same thing happening to others. People are conditioned to fear when they face a real and immediate threat—and sometimes that threat feels immediate long after it has passed. To people with anxiety disorders, post-traumatic stress, and good reason to protect themselves from trusting others, it is trite and irresponsible to say, "Just trust God." Ultimately, trust in the only one who will never do us wrong is the remedy. But learning to trust anyone—even God—may require a long time, a lot of practice, therapeutic counseling, anti-anxiety medication or other professional help. At the same time, such treatments don't replace the need for trust.

There's a difference between trusting God and trusting *in* God. We need to do both. For an illustration of what it means to practice trust in God, try this exercise: Read a few verses that depict the nurturing motherly love God has for his children (Num 11:12; Job 38:8-9; Ps 36:7; Is 46:3-4; 49:15-16; 66:13; Mt 23:37). Then be still and imagine you are lying in the arms of God, as a baby lies in its mother's arms. There is nothing babies can do to find or prepare their next meal. They are completely helpless, yet they don't even know how vulnerable they would be without their parents' care. Worrying wouldn't make babies safer, happier, healthier or more capable of providing for themselves. All they can reasonably do is make their needs known and trust in loving people to provide. Try to adopt that same attitude toward your own heavenly parent, who is far more capable, wise, strong and loving than you can imagine.

For most of the passages I've described in this chapter, we rarely frame them as warnings against worry and affirmations of what the people involved learned about God and his trustworthiness. We focus on character traits, try to find positive ways we can emulate the people involved. And when they don't seem worthy of emulation, sometimes we roll our eyes at these ancient people, who found it so hard to trust God despite their "easy" spiritual lives—after all, God was appearing in clouds, flames and dreams. He spoke from bright lights, burning bushes and the mouths of prophets. How could they not trust a God who made himself so obvious? It's a question worth pondering.

5

No Easy Life

Sometimes when we read the Bible through our lenses, colored and misshapen by thousands of geographical miles and thousands of years of history, we're tempted to believe that God's ancient people somehow had it easier than we do—they didn't have so much to worry about; they didn't face the kinds of temptations we do; they heard and saw the miraculous on so many occasions. Sure, God expected them to trust him implicitly, but it's understandable for us to struggle a bit more. We have so much less assurance and so much more to worry about . . . or do we?

Let's take a closer look at just four of the Scripture passages listed in the last chapter and consider their circumstantial context. God clearly expected trust from the people in each of them—against backdrops that were not as easy as we like to imagine.

THE ISRAELITES STAND TRAPPED BETWEEN THE RED SEA AND EGYPT'S ARMY—EXODUS 14:10-18

When the Israelites find themselves facing the Red Sea, with Pharaoh's pursuing army at their backs, they have plenty of reasons to panic. And contrary to what we like to believe about them, they had very little personal historical experience that would motivate them to trust God in this situation.

The "Israelites," as we now call them, were not a nation at this time. They had never had their own homeland, sense of national identity, political or even religious leaders. Israel was not the name of a country or nationality; it was a family name. This group of people was the descendants of one man, Jacob, to whom God had given the name Israel. They had traveled to the land of Egypt as one extended family, a total of around seventy people, to escape a severe regional famine. They had been welcomed, fed and granted land by a generous Pharaoh and his right-hand man, Jacob's favored son Joseph. They had settled in, quickly multiplied and spent 215 years growing into a people who remained distinct from their Egyptian neighbors, first because they were geographically isolated and eventually because they were enslaved.

So when the highly unusual Moses—a child of Israel but raised in Pharaoh's palace—came walking out of the desert, telling his relatives it was time to leave, he was calling them to a terrifying course of action. He told them Yahweh—who may have seemed to abandon them at least a couple of generations ago—was telling them to walk away from the only home they had known and set across the desert for a land they had never seen. These were people who had been born in Egypt, many of them born into slavery, and who had learned to survive in a system they resented but didn't actively resist. They were used to being told where they could live, how they could spend their time and even whether their newborn children would be allowed to live.

For roughly the same number of years that the United States of America has been in existence, the people of Israel had lived in Egypt. Their "founding fathers" were long dead, and while the stories of their ancestors had survived, their sense of destiny and promise must have been latent at best.

Nonetheless, their elders had been convinced by Moses and his more eloquent brother, Aaron. They had responded in worship when they saw the miraculous signs God did through Moses. They had believed Moses when he told them Yahweh saw them, cared about them and was about to deliver them (Ex 4:29-31). But after Pharaoh responded by increasing their workload, the Israelite foremen confronted Moses and Aaron and blamed them for their hardship. And Moses in turn confronted God—after all, the trouble had started with him, and Moses wondered why God hadn't yet followed through on his promise to deliver them from Egypt (Ex 5:19-23).

This became a pattern—Moses' bold confrontation of Pharaoh, followed by repercussions, followed by the people's questioning of Moses, followed by Moses' questioning of God. It indicates a plague of uncertainty and insecurity among the people of Israel—the same thing any of us would feel if someone told us God had promised to improve our lives and instead our lives seemed to get steadily worse.

So now, having left Egypt with their former oppressors' riches in hand, the people of Israel find that things have become much, much worse. They are marching through the wilderness, following one man and a cloud, on a roundabout way to a place they have only heard about in stories. Camped along the seashore, they suddenly realize Pharaoh's army is pursuing them. Their Egyptian taskmasters, abusers, intimidators want them back, and they can't escape because they have stupidly walked right into a trap. They have no army, no governors, no diplomats to intervene.

They panic, which is a completely natural thing to do. They see overwhelming evidence that they have followed Moses on a suicide mission (Ex 14:10-12). They remember how Moses' fancy ideas about freedom have caused trouble before, and they wish they had never left Egypt.

Moses' response is to give the most ridiculous, counterintuitive command he could have: "Don't be afraid. Just stand still and watch" (Ex 14:13). If ever there was a time for "fight or flight," this is it. And they are supposed to stand still.

What comes next is an incredible faith-building experience that reverberates through generations. But what God asks them to do—stand still and expect him to fight for them—is a tremendous act of faith in a God they barely know. They don't have the Holy Spirit indwelling them, teaching them and assuring them of God's presence. They don't yet have priests, a temple or even the tabernacle to represent God's presence. There is no sacrificial system to pay for sin, no set of laws to follow, no written record of God's character. And aside from the miraculous signs done by Moses and a series of really bad things that happened to the Egyptians and seemed to undermine their gods, they have no real assurance that they have a special relationship with God. There they stand in terror and hysteria, resigned to reenslavement or death.

I'm sure this is not easy—and I'm not sure everyone truly trusted God at that point. But God certainly asks them to do so, and he asks us to do the same thing in our circumstances.

THE ASSYRIAN ARMY THREATENS JERUSALEM—ISAIAH 30

When King Hezekiah tries to make an alliance with Egypt, seeking help against the Assyrian army, he is not imagining a threat. The threat is real, imminent and terrifying.

King Hezekiah's predecessor (and father), King Ahaz, had forged an alliance with the Assyrian empire, subjugating Judah to Assyria in exchange for protection. This meant Judah was required to pay tribute to Assyria. When Hezekiah came into power, he made a host of dramatic changes in his kingdom. Among them, he rebelled against the Assyrian king, Sennacherib, refusing to continue to pay (2 Kings 18:7).

The consequence of this choice became clear when Sennacherib and his army came marching toward Jerusalem, destroying other cities in Judah along the way. As they approached, Hezekiah got worried, changed his mind and offered Sennacherib tribute in exchange for withdrawal. In fact, he looted the treasuries of the palace and the temple and even pulled off the gold overlaying the doors and doorposts of the temple. But though he sent all this treasure to Sennacherib, the army still approached.

Many of Judah's leaders decide to take action by forging an alliance with Egypt. They send a caravan of gifts to Egypt to secure Egypt's help in repelling the Assyrian attack. This is in direct rebellion against what God, through Isaiah, told them to do. What did he instruct them to do instead? "Only in returning to me and resting in me will you be saved. In quietness and confidence is your strength" (Is 30:15).

Quietness and confidence? Repentance? Easier said than done, especially with a large army raising dust within your borders. The Assyrian army had already sacked the kingdom of Israel (2 Kings 18:10). Now they had destroyed the outlying cities of Judah. They had the ability to make quick work of Jerusalem, and they were eager to do so.

Hezekiah sends three of his officials to negotiate with Assyrian officials just outside Jerusalem's wall. There Sennacherib's chief of staff taunted Jerusalem, proclaiming loudly that Assyria would destroy them, and ridiculed their faith in both Egypt and God. Hezekiah's officials ask the Assyrian not to speak in Hebrew, because they don't want the people to hear what he says. But he does so intentionally, and the people of Jerusalem hear his mockery:

> But Sennacherib's chief of staff replied, "Do you think my master sent this message only to you and your master? He wants all the people to hear it, for when we put this city under siege, they will suffer along with you. They will be so hungry and thirsty that they will eat their own dung and drink their own urine."
>
> Then the chief of staff stood and shouted in Hebrew to the people on the wall, "Listen to this message from the great king of Assyria! This is what the king says: Don't let Hezekiah deceive you. He will never be able to rescue you from my power. Don't let him fool you into trusting in the LORD by saying, 'The

Lord will surely rescue us. This city will never fall into the hands of the Assyrian king!'

"Don't listen to Hezekiah! These are the terms the king of Assyria is offering: Make peace with me—open the gates and come out. Then each of you can continue eating from your own grapevine and fig tree and drinking from your own well. Then I will arrange to take you to another land like this one—a land of grain and new wine, bread and vineyards, olive groves and honey. Choose life instead of death!

"Don't listen to Hezekiah when he tries to mislead you by saying, 'The Lord will rescue us!' Have the gods of any other nations ever saved their people from the king of Assyria? What happened to the gods of Hamath and Arpad? And what about the gods of Sepharvaim, Hena, and Ivvah? Did any god rescue Samaria from my power? What god of any nation has ever been able to save its people from my power? So what makes you think that the Lord can rescue Jerusalem from me?" (2 Kings 18:27-35)

This is a compelling speech; these were not empty threats. The Assyrian army might look small and weak through the lenses of history and modern warfare, but they were fierce, relentless and absolutely dominant at this time.

The people of Jerusalem who peer over the wall stare at the formidable forces of the military superpower of their day. The Assyrians had terrorized the region for more than five hundred years, partly because fighting was pretty much what the Assyrians were about. They were early innovators in chariot combat, fighting on horseback and iron weaponry; they used iron weapons when everyone else was using bronze. They were known for their brutality: cutting off limbs, flaying captured soldiers, burning them alive, flooding conquered cities and making pyramids outside the cities they destroyed—pyramids built from the skulls of the people they slaughtered. They were also fond of the siege, another area where they exercised innovation. They were pioneers in the use of battering rams and siege towers, so even fortified cities (like Jerusalem) were not safe when the Assyrian army approached. They had a bad reputation, and their empire was built on fear.

Isaiah tells the people of Jerusalem, and their leaders, to turn to God, repent of their sin, then wait on God to deliver them. The kingdom's leaders panic and even tell people not to listen to prophets like Isaiah:

> They tell the seers,
>   "Stop seeing visions!"
> They tell the prophets,
>   "Don't tell us what is right.
> Tell us nice things.
>   Tell us lies.
> Forget all this gloom.
>   Get off your narrow path.
> Stop telling us about your
>   'Holy One of Israel.'" (Is 30:10-11)

Do you think it was easy for King Hezekiah and his people to trust God and wait like the proverbial sitting ducks? God knew what he was asking of them, and he knows what he's asking of us as well. What would you have done if you'd looked out your kitchen window and seen the Assyrian army approaching? What will you do with the fears that are staring you down today?

JESUS TELLS PEOPLE NOT TO WORRY—MATTHEW 6

Although the Bible doesn't tell us where the Sermon on the Mount took place, tradition places this event on a hillside along the shore of the Sea of Galilee, between Tabgha and Capernaum in what is now northern Israel. Regardless of exactly where Jesus spoke these words, he was addressing people—both Jews and Gentiles—who lived in first-century Palestine.

The people lived under Roman rule, in a small but troublesome region of the Roman Empire. The mighty Romans never could figure out how to get along peacefully with the people who lived in Palestine, and the people never accepted Roman rule. The Jews' monotheistic beliefs contrasted sharply with the polytheistic Roman religious system, and their sense of identity as a set-apart people rubbed Rome the wrong way. Although the area was directly ruled by King Herod and his sons, who were partly Jewish, these rulers represented Rome and were seen as traitors by the people under their government.

Within the Jewish world, this was a time of religious disunity, with loyalties divided among four main sects: Pharisees, Sadducees, Zealots and Essenes. Most first-century Jews were restless, believing they were still in exile, still suffering under the thumb of pagans because of their past rebellion against God. They were eager for God's promised Messiah, whom they counted on to restore their nation and deliver them from their Roman oppressors.

Ninety percent of the population was peasants, and all were oppressively taxed to support a small number of elites and to pay for the Roman oversight they hated so much. While some worked as builders and carpenters, fishermen, weavers, leather workers, tax collectors and other tradesmen, nearly all people sustained themselves through subsistence-level agriculture of some kind. All their work was physically intense. Farmers did their work manually with the assistance of animals like donkeys and oxen. Shepherds had to keep constant vigilance over their flocks, even sleeping with them out in the open.

Folks were utterly dependent on rain and favorable weather. They ate simple foods—mainly bread, which provided most of their caloric intake. They typically also ate olives, onions and grapes, and a little of other foods like vegetables, legumes, fish and cheese. But even such a simple diet required hard work. Gathering water and preparing food were perpetual jobs. Food-preservation techniques were primitive compared to modern refrigeration and even canning methods. They would not have been able to conceive of what we now take for granted—a large storehouse of prepared food readily available for purchase and waiting to be eaten at their convenience. There was no simple turning on a faucet to get a drink of cold water.

Likewise, the idea of a closet full of ready-made clothes, purchased whimsically with little thought to how they were made, would have been preposterous. They had far more reason to worry about what to eat, drink or wear than we do. By contrast, we all have an embarrassment of riches and a luxury of leisure. In fact, most of us are more worried about curbing our appetites than satisfying our basic needs.

The people of first-century Palestine did not find it any easier to trust God with their basic needs than we do. In fact, they lived in the shadow of starvation and death all the time. If Jesus told these ancient people not to worry about food, drink and clothes, what does he expect of us, who have so much more?

PETER TELLS EARLY CHRISTIANS HOW TO ENDURE PERSECUTION—1 PETER 3

First Peter is a letter attributed to the apostle Peter, written to followers of Christ (converted Jews and Gentiles) in northern Asia Minor, in what is now Turkey. These early believers, living in the Roman Empire, were suffering persecution. Since this letter was likely written between A.D. 60 and 65, their suffering probably was not a result of official state-sponsored persecution, sanctioned by the Roman Empire. Such persecution came later, starting around A.D. 250.

But that doesn't make these Christians' suffering any less real. At this time, Christians were subject to suspicion and social persecution, often in response to popular misunderstandings about this new religious movement. Christians were rumored to engage in unsavory rites such as cannibalism and orgies. They were suspected of plotting to overthrow the Roman government. Their simple and communal life aroused suspicion. They were believed to be atheists because they didn't worship the Roman gods. And because Christians didn't appease the Roman gods by worshiping them, Romans believed they made the gods angry, and the gods responded with natural disasters and other calamities for which the Christians were to blame. This made Christians targets of resentment when such hardships hit.

In addition, because Christians were already despised, they made a convenient scapegoat when the emperor Nero needed someone to take the heat for a fire that burned 70 percent of Rome in A.D. 64. People initially pointed the finger at Nero for the catastrophic fire, which lasted more than a week. So Nero deflected the blame toward the Christians, whom society already eyed with suspicion and hatred. He executed hundreds of them, burning them alive, crucifying them and allowing them to be dismembered by wild animals in the arena. This sparked an increase in social persecution, which eventually (more than 150 years later) erupted into systematic state-sponsored persecution that lasted for two hundred years.

Roman law left many gaps in defining what was and was not legal. Therefore, before Rome officially declared Christians enemies of the state, governors of outlying districts were free to prosecute crimes at their own discretion. So more severe persecution did happen sporadically and locally. Christians apparently were treated more harshly—even executed—in some places simply because the governor of that region had decided it was a crime to be a Christian.

If anyone understood persecution, it was Peter. He was beaten, threatened, punished and jailed for preaching the gospel of Jesus. He died a martyr's death at the hands of Nero not long after this letter was written, in A.D. 67 or 68. He knew what it meant to endure without bitterness and without losing hope. He knew how to live under the constant threat of harm and even death. He also knew how to live an obedient, victorious life by faith.

Peter encourages the believers to patiently endure suffering and to make their lives exemplary, being sure they were suffering for doing good, not for doing wrong. He encourages them to put their trust in God and to pay people back with blessing rather than retaliation. He tells them, "Don't worry or be afraid of their threats" (1 Pet 3:14). He tells them to follow the example of Jesus, who "did not retaliate when he was insulted, nor threaten revenge when he suffered. He left his case in the hands of God, who always judges fairly" (1 Pet 2:23).

These Christians were not simply enduring a ribbing at the hands of late-night talk show hosts or the writers of *Saturday Night Live*. They weren't just socially unpopular or holding minority opinions on political or social issues. They weren't living among people who went to church only on Christmas and Easter, or wrestling over how to adjust to an increasingly pluralistic society. They had no political power; they were not members of the world's most widespread religion as we are.

They were small communities of people who had recently embraced a brand-new view of the world, surrounded by a pagan and polytheistic culture. They found themselves suddenly at odds with their friends and their family members. There were no Christian media, Christian schools, Christian books, Christian conferences and camps to encourage them, help them consider how Christianity might inform their worldview and connect them to a worldwide movement of the Holy Spirit. They were in true danger, objects of misunderstanding and seething resentment that laid a foundation for official persecution throughout their sprawling and brutally powerful empire.

Yet these early Christians weren't supposed to worry. And neither are we, who live such safe and comfortable lives by comparison.

WORRY HOLDS US BACK

I hope these glimpses behind the curtain have shattered the myth that ancient people found it easier to trust God. God's call for his people to trust him was as difficult—and as sensible—then as it is today. The sensational displays of God's power described in the

Bible may seem to us as though they happened all the time, because they are collected and familiar. But like us, most people throughout history, even ancient history, never saw such faith-bolstering events. They believed based on the stories they knew and on their own experience of God in the mundane. The people whose stories are told in our Scriptures had plenty of reasons for worry, but God called them to be countercultural in living through trust in him. He calls us to do the same.

In many ways, we can relate to what these ancient sisters and brothers experienced. But in other ways, we can't imagine how difficult their lives were—just as they would not have been able to imagine the complexity of our world. In the face of such hardship, God told them to turn away from fear and worry and to trust him instead. It is not unreasonable to believe he wants us to do so as well. God cares as much about our faith and worry as he did about theirs. Worry is a tremendous obstacle to the bold and sacrificial life he has called us to. Like all sin, it offends God and impairs our relationship with him.

We, who are among the most comfortable Christians in history, have no business embracing fear and letting worry drain us of the strength God gives. It's time for us to repent of worry, recognize we can make a different choice, and pursue the frightening freedom and baffling peace of trust in God.

This is not about simply "handing our worries over to God"; it's about understanding how incredibly powerful and trustworthy God is, how much higher his ways are than ours, how ridiculous it is for us to cling to the illusion of control and the fear of what is small in God's view. It's about putting our concerns in their proper place, in relationship to God's concerns. It's about who God is, not who we are. It means taking seriously Paul's instruction to "let God transform you into a new person by changing the way you think" (Rom 12:2).

True repentance from worry also means embracing a willingness to sacrifice. It's one thing to say, "I will take a risk to follow Jesus, and God will protect me from harm." It's quite another thing to say, "I will take a risk to follow Jesus, and God might or might not protect me from harm. I will do it anyway and accept the possibility that it will cost me tremendously." This calls for letting go, rather than clinging to our own safety and comforts.

It means following the example of Shadrach, Meshach and Abednego, who told the mighty King Nebuchadnezzar of Babylon, "If we are thrown into the blazing furnace, the God whom we serve is able to save us. He will rescue us from your power, Your Majesty. *But even if he doesn't,* we want to make it clear to you, Your Majesty, that we will never serve your gods or worship the gold statue you have set up" (Dan 3:17-18, emphasis added). These young men had not seen the mighty hand of God at work on behalf of their nation; they had known only his discipline, in response to their great sin, resulting in captivity in Babylon. Yet they had heard the stories of God's relationship with their people and had experienced his goodness in their exile. And they chose to trust him—and to accept death before unfaithfulness to God.

It means following the example of Christians like Catherine of Siena, who survived the Black Death as a young child, then as an adult faced another wave of the horrifying plague as it ravaged Western Europe. She and her followers refused to flee Siena when the plague arrived, instead staying and risking their lives to minister to the sick and bury the dead. Their service in the name of Christ was more important than preserving their lives.

It means heeding the words of Jesus, who told his disciples as he commissioned them for ministry, "If you cling to your life, you will lose it; but if you give up your life for me, you will find it" (Mt 10:39).

It means recognizing that we serve this same God who asked his people to trust him through horrifying circumstances and who asks us to do the same. It means realizing that God's power, strength and faithfulness do not diminish with the passing of time, and his goodness is not diminished by our circumstances. It means embracing the unknown that is very much known to God—and in the process, letting go of what we are so tempted to cling to. It means standing out in this world, marked by our courage in the face of that which threatens our bodies but can't destroy our souls (Matthew 10:28).

God wants us to be as bright, inviting and easy to find as "a city on a hilltop that cannot be hidden" (Mt 5:14). He calls us to live differently—not because of anything we do, but because he has dramatically changed us. Because he has redeemed us from hopelessness, given us a glimpse of life way beyond this one, and graced us with purpose and a reason to live. But many of us are instead cowering in corners and counting stitches on quilts of worry, which will never keep us warm. We need a new, refreshed perspective.

Affirm Your Faith

Before we take a closer look at a different perspective, I want to acknowledge that as your perspective changes, you may be tempted to believe your problems with worry have vanished. While a new perspective is essential for the kind of mental transformation that can result in habitual trust, such a perspective doesn't mean worry will never beckon again. In fact, I'm completely certain you will be tempted to worry nearly every day.

So what can you do when that temptation calls? You can start by reminding yourself where you place your trust. Try personalizing a passage of Scripture that can serve as your statement of commitment to the way of faith and trust in the one who holds all things in his hand. Memorize it and recite it when your heart is troubled. For example, you might personalize Habakkuk 3:17-19, changing the calamities to reflect the things that worry you, as a way to reaffirm your faith and trust in God regardless of your circumstances.

My version of Habakkuk 3:17-19 might say something like this:

Even though my children go hungry and die, and my husband becomes incapacitated by illness or accident; even though I lose my faculties and my ability to care for the ones I love; even though there is no money in the bank and no one to enforce justice, yet I will rejoice in the Lord! I will be joyful in the God of my salvation! The Sovereign Lord is my strength! He gives me confidence that his way is right and makes me strong enough to live his way no matter what the circumstances; he gives me joy and assurance and hope regardless of what I can see.

Here's another idea: Find a partner to act as your "worry sponsor." Share your statement of faith affirmation with this person. Talk about your commitment to trust God. Then call the person for encouragement when you're tempted to give in to worry.

Over the next three chapters, we'll look at three things that keep us clinging to worry: a faulty perspective, a desire to possess and control the future, and a possessive attachment to the people and things of this world.

6

It's All About Perspective

If you recognize that you have a problem with worry and that it inhibits your relationship with God—not to mention your life of mission and purpose in response to God's grace—you probably want to change. You may think the best way to stop worrying is simply to exercise greater self-discipline and will power. While both practices can help us change our habits, the most powerful thing we can do is allow God to change what we believe about him. If we're going to turn away from worry, we need to treat the heart of the problem: our theology. Here's why: A new perspective can have tremendous transformative power in our lives.

THE POWER OF CHANGING OUR MINDS

I'm married to a counselor, so when my husband and I talk about his work, I hear a lot about theories and approaches to helping people. In the world of mental-health treatment, one increasingly popular (and demonstrably effective) therapeutic method is cognitive-behavioral therapy. Therapists who use this approach, like my husband, focus less on helping people change their behaviors, emotions and circumstances, and more on helping them change their thoughts. This is because they believe behaviors and emotions don't occur in a vacuum; our thoughts and beliefs are ultimately responsible for our behaviors and feelings. As the National Association of Cognitive-Behavioral Therapists describes it, "Cognitive-behavioral therapy is based on the idea that our *thoughts* cause our feelings and behaviors, not external things, like people, situations, and events. The benefit of this fact is that we can change the way we think to feel/act better even if the situation does not change."[1]

Of course, our behaviors (especially habits) influence our thoughts as well, and cognitive-behavioral therapists also encourage clients to make positive choices that will help them live healthier lives and reinforce their belief in things that are true. But ultimately, our choices reflect what's happening in our minds.

This is a very biblical concept. In the words of Jesus:

Anything you eat passes through the stomach and then goes into the sewer. But the words you speak come from the heart—that's what defiles you. For from the heart come evil thoughts, murder, adultery, all sexual immorality, theft, lying, and slander. These are what defile you. Eating with unwashed hands will never defile you. (Mt 15:17-20)

"Guard your heart above all else," the wisdom of Proverbs tells us, "for it determines the course of your life" (Prov 4:23).

Paul had a few things to say on the subject. He told the Roman church,

Those who are dominated by the sinful nature think about sinful things, but those who are controlled by the Holy Spirit think about things that please the Spirit. So letting your sinful nature control your mind leads to death. But letting the Spirit control your mind leads to life and peace. (Rom 8:5-6)

A few chapters later in the same letter, Paul described the way Christ changes his followers: "Don't copy the behavior and customs of this world, but let God transform you into a new person by changing the way you think. Then you will learn to know God's will for you, which is good and pleasing and perfect" (Rom 12:2).

And in his letter to the Philippian church, Paul affirmed the importance of disciplined thinking: "Fix your thoughts on what is true, and honorable, and right, and pure, and lovely, and admirable. Think about things that are excellent and worthy of praise" (Phil 4:8).

The idea behind cognitive-behavioral therapy has strong scientific support as well, including in the booming scientific frontier of human brain research, even spawning a new field called neurotheology. In their 2009 book *How God Changes Your Brain,* neurotheology pioneer Andrew Newberg and therapist Mark Robert Waldman use neuroscience to establish this startling concept: belief in God—and religious activity itself—physically changes our brains. This is true regardless of the religious system one follows. And more specifically, "If a belief in God provides you with a sense of comfort and security, then God will enhance your life. But if you see God as a vindictive deity who gives you justification for inflicting harm on others, such a belief can actually damage your brain as it motivates you to act in socially destructive ways."[2]

The authors devote a chapter to the destructive power of fear and anger—particularly when religiously based. They describe patients who respond to disease with the assumption that they're suffering because God is punishing them:

> They first ask the question, "Why me?" They wonder if God is angry at them, and they often ruminate on guilt. . . . Research has shown that religious fear and guilt can evoke feelings of depression and thoughts of suicide, particularly for people who believe they have committed an unforgivable sin. Often, logic

and medical reasoning has little effect on these patients. However, most university hospitals have come to realize that for many patients, the problem is as much a spiritual issue as a medical one.[3]

The solution is the same as God's prescription: faith. "Faith tempers our anxiety and fears, and it may even temper one's belief in an angry God. The beauty of Job's story is that it reminds the suffering believer that God is ultimately compassionate. And from the perspective of medicine and neuroscience, compassion can heal the body as well as the soul."[4]

In his illuminating book, *The God-Shaped Brain,* Christian psychiatrist Timothy R. Jennings also helps readers understand how our beliefs about God, true or untrue, change our brains. He explains how fear—the kind of ongoing fear we embrace when we worry—shapes our brains destructively:

> The constant firing of the anxiety system occurs in brains out of balance and is an overreaction to environmental stimuli. Because of sin, all of our brains are out of balance and we all experience, far too frequently, the effects of out-of-control stress, the amygdala [what he refers to as "the fear center of the brain"] firing. Evolutionary biologists would suggest that the fight-or-flight response is a very adaptive reaction to promote survival in the face of immediate crisis. But it is the firing of this alarm system that damages the brain, impairs healthy thinking and abuses the body. The longer the alarm fires, the more pronounced the damage.[5]

In chapter three, I described several ways worry hurts us. In his book, Dr. Jennings describes how these effects of ongoing stress look in our brains. They damage special white cells that surround, protect and nurture our neurons and the amazing structures that link them to one another. They impede the production of proteins that feed our existing neurons and help us create new ones.[6] So as we spend more of our lives in a state of fear, anxiety and stress, our neurons don't function as well as they should and we decrease production of healthy new ones.

But while these effects cause all kinds of secondary problems, including depression and other disorders, these effects are not irreversible. "The good news is that many brain regions remain changeable throughout life, thanks to a condition called neuroplasticity. This is particularly true of the prefrontal cortex. As we exercise healthy neural circuits, these circuits develop, strengthen and expand. Conversely, the brain prunes unhealthy circuits when we leave them idle." He goes on to talk about God's methods for increasing brain health and nurturing mental stability. "And what are God's methods? Truth, love and freedom."[7]

It's amazing how a shaft of God's truth can change our perspective. With a glimpse of eternity, today's challenges suddenly grow "strangely dim." This doesn't mean we're called to live like ostriches, determinedly burying our heads in the sand. As one friend said, "I prefer the real world to trying to live in a cave somewhere. Jesus didn't come to save us into a cave-life. He came to invite us into the kingdom-life." Trusting God doesn't require us to deny reality— that's hypocrisy and cowardice. True trust allows us to acknowledge trouble, pain and danger as we recognize God's great shadow looming over all of it.

God's truth can physically change our brains. And changing our minds changes our habits—including our emotional habits. Changing our theology, or embracing a more impressive view of God based on what God has revealed through Scripture, can transform us emotionally. It can build our faith and inspire greater trust. It can help us overcome or minimize a problem with worry. So a healthy dose of healing truth is what I aim to give you next.

GOOD THINGS TO KNOW

If we're going to change our minds, and ultimately our habits, we can start by reviewing some catalytic things God wants us to know about himself. Embracing worry rather than trust ultimately comes down to a lack of recognition of our true place in the world. Like Adam and Eve, we want to believe we're capable of more than we are and in control of more than we can possibly handle. An inflated view of ourselves doesn't leave enough room for the truth about God and our dependence on him. We need to reorient ourselves with a proper perspective on who we are, who God is and why only God is worthy of our trust.

God is unlimited. God is not limited in any way, and certainly not by the boundaries of what we can and cannot understand or envision. He is not bound by the constraints of space, time or the physical laws he created. He never wonders what to do, speculates about the future or feels threatened by human activity.

"My thoughts are nothing like your thoughts," says the LORD.
    "And my ways are far beyond anything you could imagine.
For just as the heavens are higher than the earth,
    so my ways are higher than your ways
    and my thoughts higher than your thoughts." (Is 55:8-9)

A focus on God's strength—indeed, his very nature—reveals our worried attempts at control as ridiculous. Do we actually think we know better than he does how to unfold the future or navigate the present? He knows all, sees all, is unlimited by all boundaries and concepts. Do we really believe this? Can we not trust him?

God has plans of his own. God's plans can unravel our careful planning in an instant. We're surprised by job losses, job opportunities, political realities, family crises, people who need our help, unexpected deaths, unplanned pregnancies, new relationships, scientific discoveries, new ideas and fresh dreams. We think we need to hold on to relationships because we can envision a future in them; the future may unfold quite differently. (I'm really glad I didn't end up married to any of the boys I thought were so perfect for me when I was a teenager.) When we were children, you and I thought we would someday be astronauts, firefighters, professional athletes, doctors, nurses and circus performers. Now we spend our lives doing all kinds of other things (and I'm glad that not everyone who thought they would be a doctor actually practices medicine today).

Life also has a way of popping the stitches on what we think we have sewn up. Several years ago, my husband and I bought a big house we thought we would grow into and finish raising our children in. It seemed to make sense at the time, but less than two years later, we moved one thousand miles away right before the housing bubble burst in the United States. As the Great Recession developed and wore on, we were saddled with that house, which drained us financially and emotionally. After five and a half years, we spent our entire savings to make it attractive to buyers. We finally sold it for a price that allowed us to walk away without spending any more money on it—but didn't allow us to regain a single dollar of the tens of thousands we had poured into it over nearly eight years. We were broke.

While financial analysts could have predicted what happened in our economy and how it affected people like us (and we later found out some had), we could not have known what was coming. But God certainly knew. And rather than somehow prevent us from purchasing the house or moving to a new state and new jobs, he used these circumstances to teach us some powerful lessons about faith, trust, wisdom and the fleeting value of material possessions.

God's concerns are more important than ours. God's priorities and ours don't always coincide. In fact, they usually don't. We have a very small perspective, rooted mostly in our own personal stories. God is writing a much greater and grander story, which started before the dawn of human history and which features him as the main character.

It's ridiculous for us to insist on our way, to expect that life should unfold as we think it should. It's also pointless.

God is good. Do you really believe this? Do you understand that the presence of unspeakable evil in this world does not mean God is not good? Look around you and see all the goodness he sustains. In his mercy and his unfathomable love, he has not destroyed us despite our corruption (and for all our potential and our good intentions, human corruption is hard to deny). He is executing a brilliantly good plan to rescue us from ourselves and restore the world as it should be. He is good, and we can trust that his plans are always good, even if they don't match what we want.

We often think like young children, who equate goodness with pleasure, sweetness and comfort. From this point of view, parents might seem evil for depriving their kids of pleasure, sweetness and comfort by limiting sugar intake, making them go to school, and requiring them to go to bed at night and get up in the morning. But good parents have another definition of goodness, and our plans for our children are good, even if they don't understand and don't always get to live the kind of life they want to. This is even more true for us in relationship to God: not getting what we want is not a legitimate reason to question whether God is good. Neither is reaping the consequences of our own choices. This is true even when what we want is simply a life free of serious pain and suffering. We long for a world without excruciating suffering—and this longing is good; we were made for a better world and someday will live in one. But the presence of suffering in this world is caused by sin, not by God. And believing God should regularly rescue and shield us from the consequences of sin in this world means that in looking for relief, we have misunderstood the destructive power of our own condition and lost sight of God's glorious and permanent rescue plan and redemptive power.

God calls us to joy. Jesus said, "When you obey my commandments, you remain in my love, just as I obey my Father's commandments and remain in his love. I have told you these things so that you will be filled with my joy. Yes, your joy will overflow!" (Jn 15:10-11).

Philippians 4:4 calls us to "always be full of joy in the Lord. I say it again—rejoice!"

Galatians 5:22 tells us that joy is one type of "fruit" the presence of God's Holy Spirit produces in our lives. James 1:2-3 tells us our call toward joy is not dependent on circumstance—we are to have joy even in the midst of suffering.

This joy God calls us to is different from the fleeting and circumstantial happiness we are tempted to pursue. It's a deeper and more mysterious experience that happens when our spirits are in right relationship with God. Such joy is not a given for Christians—it can be disrupted by sin and by things like our choices to pursue the world's cheap happiness instead.

How can we live abundantly, joyfully, when we're consumed by worry? Yet that's the way God wants us to live in spite of the condition of this world. He isn't stupid or delusional. He knows better than we do how poisonous our world is. To live with joy and contentment, trusting God with the present and the future, is a countercultural feat that can be accomplished only through him. This brings him glory.

God calls us to peace. Peace is another byproduct of the Holy Spirit's work in us and our choice to remain in step with that work. As with joy, Jesus extends us his peace and wants us to live in it. And it's dramatically different from what the world can give us (Jn 14:27; Phil 4:7). But it's impossible to be at peace and worried at the same time.

God calls us to trust. God doesn't tell us everything we want to know. He doesn't clear all obstacles from our path or take away our choices. He has not promised to make life easy for us. He has placed us in this challenging world at a complex time, and he wants us to trust him. Sometimes that means we believe him when everything happening around us tells us God is a liar. "For we live by believing and not by seeing" (2 Cor 5:7). Sometimes it means we're still when our instincts tell us it's our job to take action (Ps 46:10). There is no better way for us to learn that without God, we're hopeless and helpless to do anything that really matters (Jn 15:5).

Trust does not mean we will be happy or that "it will all work out in the end." It doesn't mean life will be neat and tidy or we'll always feel like thanking God for what comes our way. My friend learned more about this when she was pregnant with her first child and a second-trimester ultrasound indicated the possibility that her baby would be born with severe brain problems. She and her husband endured "three horrible months when we had to face the reality that things can (and do) turn out bad for Christians sometimes. That all the clichés well-meaning Christians at our church were telling us were false. That trusting God will not make everything turn out okay; it means knowing that we may not get the answer to prayer we want."

God knows where we live. When God calls us to trust him, he is not being naive. He knows what kind of world we live in, and he knows better than we do how disappointing it can be. In fact, we're the ones who are often naive in our expectations. Our culture of worry is informed by our misguided understanding that ease and prosperity are normal conditions that God somehow owes us.

Instead, we should expect trouble, as Jesus promised his followers before his assurance that he has overcome the world (Jn 16:33). God knows we will have hardship. We are not here to avoid pain or simply to seek our own pleasure. While we're here, in "this life that is dominated by sin and death" (Rom 7:24), we will never have the safe, comfortable, perfect life we want. And if we did achieve the best possible life on this planet, we would be settling for so much less than what God offers us. Our longings are not meant to drive us toward our own comfort in this life. They're meant to drive us to Christ and to long for him and what he offers. Yet so many of our worries are fueled by our desire to make of this life what it simply cannot be.

God wants to relieve our burdens. Jesus proclaimed, "Come to me, all of you who are weary and carry heavy burdens, and I will give you rest. Take my yoke upon you. Let me teach you, because I am humble and gentle at heart, and you will find rest for your souls. For my yoke is easy to bear, and the burden I give you is light" (Mt 11:28-30). But it isn't just everyday rest he wants to give us—it's soul-deep sabbath rest, the rest from trying to save and redeem ourselves from the burden of sin. From trying to fix ourselves and this world at the same time. From trying to somehow be good enough to achieve peace.

He doesn't want us to carry the weight of the world. One of the marks of his people is this spiritual rest that can be found only in him. Such rest grants us freedom to live by faith. As my sister Cheryl told me, "It's actually very freeing to learn to give up control to God."

We aren't in control—but God is. Perhaps nothing grants us more emotional relief than remembering this dual truth: we are not in charge of the world, but that doesn't mean it's out of control. Someone far greater, more righteous and wiser than us is in charge. This is one of the reasons our worry is futile: "You can make many plans, but the LORD's purpose will prevail" (Prov 19:21).

When we rely only on our own understanding, it's easy to feel consumed with worry over the condition of our planet and the possibilities for the future of the human race. But "our God is in the heavens, and he does as he wishes" (Ps 115:3). Perhaps the most powerful Bible passage illustrating God's control over this world is Job 12, which affirms, "The life of every living thing is in his hand, and the breath of every human being" (Job 12:10).

Worry is a distraction from a life of faith and purpose. In Hebrews 12:1-2, the writer urges Christ's followers to "strip off every weight that slows us down, especially the sin that so easily trips us up . . . keeping our eyes on Jesus." Worry is a weight, and it certainly slows us down and trips us up. In fact, it has a way of pulling our eyes off Jesus as well.

God made us and knows what we need. In the context of a prophecy about Cyrus the Great and his future aid to the people of Jerusalem, through Isaiah God proclaimed,

> What sorrow awaits those who argue with their Creator.
>   Does a clay pot argue with its maker?
> Does the clay dispute with the one who shapes it, saying,
>   "Stop, you're doing it wrong!"
> Does the pot exclaim,
>   "How clumsy can you be?" (Is 45:9)

As our Creator, God truly knows us better than we know ourselves. All the mysteries of our minds, our genetic makeup, the causes and cures for diseases, our emotional lives, our senses, and our motivations are no mystery to him. In fact, Jesus said God knows every single hair on our heads (Lk 12:7). He knows what we need and gives us good gifts (Mt 7:11). He does not withhold good things from his children (Ps 84:11).

But God's definition of "good" and his understanding of what we need do not always match our own perspective. Sometimes when we worry over what we think we need, we're really trying to force the hand of the God, who said,

> Do you question what I do for my children?
>   Do you give me orders about the work of my hands?
> I am the one who made the earth
>   and created people to live on it.
> With my hands I stretched out the heavens.
>   All the stars are at my command. (Is 45:11-12)

We can't fix this world. In his excellent book *The World Is Not Ours to Save,* Tyler Wigg-Stevenson says,

> Even if every social condition were perfected (a task that I would argue is impossible), the human heart would remain catastrophically broken, "deceitful above all things and beyond cure. Who

can understand it?" (Jer 17:9). The story of our genesis tells us that a perfect people in a perfect place still failed to choose God; what hope, then, does a humanity born with congenital spiritual weakness have? Our intrinsic willingness to choose wickedness and selfishness corrupts even the best systems we can design. . . . We should not confuse our ability to undertake fundamentally *tactical* efforts—that is, working on highly specific, comprehensible problems—with an ability to transform the existential condition that gives rise to injustice in the first place. We are in trouble if that is the goal that motivates our work.[8]

While this perspective may not sound hopeful, with the embrace of this biblical truth comes tremendous hope. While we may not have the solution to our world's great illness, we do have the remedy in Christ. And while we are not free to ignore his mission for the church and for us as individuals, we are free to relinquish the responsibility we might feel to save the world. We simply are not up for it, and frankly, it's not up to us.

Ultimately, only God is worthy of fear. An old VeggieTales song proclaims, "God is bigger than the boogie man." Featuring Junior Asparagus, Larry the Cucumber and Bob the Tomato, the song was a characteristically silly and childlike way to present a very powerful concept. God is, indeed, bigger than the boogie man and all else that frightens us—even as adults.

God used the prophet Isaiah not only to speak his messages but also to serve as an example to the rest of Judah. He told Isaiah not to live in fear, as the people around him did. He said, "Make the LORD of Heaven's Armies holy in your life. He is the one you should fear. He is the one who should make you tremble. He will keep you safe" (Is 8:13-14).

Jesus himself said something similar when he told his disciples, "Don't be afraid of those who want to kill your body; they cannot touch your soul. Fear only God, who can destroy both soul and body in hell" (Mt 10:28).

When we look at our fears in light of God's power and his eternal promises to the people who live clothed in his grace, this perspective makes a lot of sense. God does not shield us from all that scares us, nor does he block all the consequences of human choices and the natural laws he created. Just because we trust in him does not mean we'll always be safe or comfortable. It doesn't mean our bodies won't be hurt or even killed. But we are always in God's hand, and ultimately he will preserve the souls he has rescued. The power of this truth may be difficult to embrace when staring into the jaws of something that threatens to swallow us whole, but it should keep us from clinging to fear and devoting ourselves to worry.

I love the classic hymn "It Is Well with My Soul." The song's lyrics were written by Horatio Spafford, an American lawyer who was inspired to write it, ironically, after he experienced some of the worst tragedies we ourselves worry about. In 1870, his four-year-old son died of pneumonia. The next year, he was financially ruined when his real estate investments were destroyed by the great fire that decimated Chicago. Two years later, an economic downturn further devastated his financial circumstances. Soon after, he sent his family on a ship to Europe, staying behind to attend to business matters. The ship collided with another vessel and sank in the Atlantic, and while his wife survived, all four of their daughters were killed.

The beauty of this song does not reside in some denial that great tragedies can and do befall people who follow Christ. Instead, its power is in the declaration that even though life can be horrifically painful, and death and decay are constant companions, our souls are in the keeping of a God who transcends all.

Only God lives in the future. As I mentioned in chapter four, much of our worry comes from trying to dwell where we cannot go: the future. That is God's domain, and we cause ourselves great grief when we try to mentally overcome the barriers that keep us in the present. I will talk more about this in the next chapter.

Nothing—and no one—belongs to us. Similarly, we create distress when we try to cling to what we don't possess. We forget that everything and everyone in this world was placed here by God; he is the only one who can create something out of nothing. We worry when we try to take God's place as lord over our loved ones, our material possessions and the potential possessions our money represents. You can read more on this idea in chapter eight.

Material comforts are fleeting. Regardless of our level of wealth, we've all grown accustomed to certain material comforts we think we can't live without. Ironically, the more of these conveniences and comforts we live with, the more reasons we have to worry about losing what we have. This is one reason some of the most physically comfortable people in the world are among the most emotionally miserable.

When we're looking for comfort, we usually look to the world around us for pleasures and possessions that soothe us for a time, until the novelty wears off or we realize our neighbors have something even better. This is a recipe for misery. We'd do much better to follow the apostle Paul's recipe: "I have learned how to be content with whatever I have. I know how to live on almost nothing or with everything. I have learned the secret of living in every situation, whether it is with a full stomach or empty, with plenty or little. For I can do everything through Christ, who gives me strength" (Phil 4:11-13).

Enjoying comfort is not inherently bad, but we will worry far less when we realize that material goods are material—and therefore destructible, losable, constantly decaying. God's care for us is not dependent on them, and they are no substitute for his care.

God does not need us. At all. Human pride is incredibly tenacious. Even those of us who recognize we cannot save ourselves and have accepted God's free gift of grace still struggle to release our determined sense that there must be some way we can pay him back, some way we can help him in return.

God's great and merciful rescue plan for humanity is not actually about humanity. It's about God himself. His love, his goodness, his perfect justice, his rich and meticulous system of symbols and signs all point back to—you guessed it—himself. We are the recipients of a kind of love, forgiveness and devastating grace that we can see and feel but can't truly understand. They change us and fill us with new purpose for our lives.

When we find that purpose, God graciously accepts our service in his name, and he infuses our clownish efforts with power and efficacy. But he doesn't need us. He doesn't save us so we can be his hard-working minions, doing the jobs he doesn't want to do or helping him get more done. He's never tired, never stymied, never insecure or short on power or creativity. He doesn't need us to stay awake at night or anticipate problems he might not see without us. He doesn't even *need* our *worship*. We need him, plain and simple. We are created by him to need him. He wants our faith, and he is powerful and kind and loving enough to offer us his peace and spiritual rest in exchange. As the great French writer Victor Hugo wrote in a letter, "Have courage for the great sorrows of life and patience for the small ones; and when you have laboriously accomplished your daily task, go to sleep in peace. God is awake."

We aren't meant to go it alone. While the Rugged Individualist may be an American hero, and the lonely superhero makes for a good Hollywood story, these models don't reflect the way we're meant to live. We are made for community and for fellowship with God. We don't have anything to prove to the one who created us, who knows our weaknesses and false fronts better than we do. Our efforts to solve our own problems, in our own ways, and carry our own burdens are pretty much pointless.

My sister Kate told me she's inspired to trust God when life's circumstances remind her how weak she is: "To know that I am so nearly powerless inspires me to trust in God as a necessity." When we come to the end of ourselves, we usually find ourselves more willing to turn to someone more powerful than we are. But we don't have to wait for life to bring us to that point. We can acknowledge our inadequacy before it overwhelms us.

"So let us come boldly to the throne of our gracious God. There we will receive his mercy, and we will find grace to help us when we need it most" (Heb 4:16). The God who made all that exists offers us his help and his peace. Why refuse?

WELCOME TRANSFORMATION

When we worry, we elevate the concerns of our kingdom above those of God's kingdom. We offend God with our lack of trust and our refusal to humbly acknowledge our position in relationship to his. We grieve him with our insistence on shouldering burdens that don't belong to us, tasting his peace but refusing a full portion.

When we keep our eyes on the world around us, we see plenty of reasons to worry. And without the assurance of God's character and his great plan for our world, there's really no reason not to worry. Yet as believers covered by his grace and living under his promise, we are called to see, live and think differently. Choosing to worry is a sin, an act of rebellion against God, a rejection of our assigned place in the universe, a barrier in our relationship with a God who wants us to live in bold purpose rooted in his character. Worry is essentially a spiritual problem, which ultimately cannot be overcome merely through an act of the will—the solution is rooted entirely in who God is.

If we believe what God tells us, we have no excuse for worry. We can trust this same God who demonstrated his power and his care for his people in the Bible. When we turn to face him, humble ourselves and allow him to transform our thinking, we find that worry is even more wasteful than we realized.

When you're motivated to worry, the following process can help reorient your perspective.

1. Acknowledge the possibilities. Admit that the future is unseen and most of life is outside your control. No matter how strong your sense of control, you will never know what waits around time's next corner.

2. Accept danger. Let go of the illusion that life can and should be safe. So much of our worry is based in our efforts to preserve safety, in defiance of the reality that we are threatened constantly. Worry binds us to the possibilities and blinds us to the truth. Acknowledge that life is not perfect, you are not safe and the worst possible things may happen to you or someone you love. Worry will not prevent these things. Live with wisdom and remember that worrying won't add a single hour to your life.

As I've freely discussed in my book *Troubled Minds: Mental Illness and the Church's Mission,* my mother has schizophrenia, a serious and chronic mental illness that often shows itself in symptomatic cycles. Like many people with schizophrenia, Mom goes through periods of time when she functions well—thanks to effective medications and healthy choices to care for herself. But eventually those stable times are followed by decline because the medication ceases to be effective or she doesn't take the dosage she needs. Inevitably, she is hospitalized, and she also behaves in ways that expose her to danger and that inconvenience, embarrass, confound or endanger others. My whole family is affected by these troubled times, and we all try to help Mom get the care she needs. But since my sister Cheryl lives nearby, a greater burden of care falls on her. And it can be a very heavy burden.

A few years ago, after a tremendously difficult period of dealing with the effects of our mother's illness, Cheryl's life got much harder. Her strong, athletic ten-year-old daughter was bitten by a tick and infected with Rocky Mountain spotted fever. She received treatment and recovered, but the disease weakened her dramatically and left her with a chronic autoimmune disorder that changed the course of her life and requires daily vigilance and care.

Not long after her daughter's initial health crisis, her husband was diagnosed with a rare autoimmune disorder as well: primary sclerosing cholangitis, which attacks the liver and can lead to, among other things, liver cancer. Doctors discovered he did have stage 3 cancer and prescribed aggressive chemotherapy and radiation treatment to give him a chance at receiving a liver transplant—the only possible treatment. He endured grueling treatments and grew desperately sick before he received the transplant that saved his life but altered it dramatically in ways that affect the whole family.

My sister, who has been through so much in recent years, told me, "I feel like the more big things that happen in my life, the less I feel the need to worry. Sometimes my worry is based on a fear of what could happen. When those things do happen, I see that God is still capable and willing to care for us even in the worst of circumstances. That takes away my doubt that he can or will in smaller circumstances."

When bad things happen, we're forced to accept the reality that they can and do happen to us. We're also trained to handle them in the future. We know we can survive, and we find hope in the way God walks us through them and redeems them as part of his glorious and loving work in this world.

3. Change your expectations. Most of us expect life to deal us a pretty good hand. When we don't get the sort of life we imagined we would, we start to worry and grow desperate to get back to what we thought was the original plan. When we expect ease and prosperity, we worry about losing them. Jesus promised, "Here on earth you will have many trials and sorrows" (Jn 16:33). When we expect trouble and thank God for blessings, our whole approach to life changes and we have fewer reasons to worry.

4. Find yourself. For us to experience peace, our sense of self and security must be divorced from what we do, what we have, even who we think we are. A few years ago, one of my friends was diagnosed with a physical defect that she apparently had had since birth, but which hadn't produced any symptoms until she was in midlife. Brain surgery was necessary, and it was risky. She was understandably nervous as she faced the possibility of paralysis, other physical injury or loss of her mental faculties. She was forced to realize that those physical and mental abilities didn't define who she was. If she were to lose them, she would still be herself, and God would not love her any less—nor would he withdraw his purpose for her life. When she came through the surgery without injury, she had all the more reason to praise God and live with that sense of purpose.

Most of us don't face such a stark challenge to our sense of self, but all of us label our identities with tags naming treasures that make us feel more valuable. Yet they can be taken from us. When we identify ourselves as God's beloved children instead, under his care and part of the family regardless of what we may gain or lose, we have fewer reasons to worry.

5. Change your point of view. Try looking at your situation through someone else's eyes. What would this problem look like to someone who lived a long time ago? To someone who lives in another part of the world? To you if your child were facing a similar problem? If you were the owner of an ant farm and the ants were obsessing about a situation like yours?

This may help you see a new way to address the problem, and it may remind you that God, who never worries, has a perspective very different from our own: "When I look at the night sky and see the work of your fingers—the moon and the stars you set in place—what are mere mortals that you should think about them, human beings that you should care for them?" (Ps 8:3-4). The problem that seems so big to you does not intimidate him.

6. Focus on what God thinks is important. Cultivate an eternal perspective—put today in its proper place. Ask yourself, *What does God think is most important here and now, where I am?* When you have your answer, focus on that and ask God to help you fulfill your mission in that moment. Your worries may fade in comparison.

For example, on a recent cross-country train trip, I sensed God urging me to turn away from the travel anxiety that typically plagues me and instead focus on the people around me. When I did, I found ways to extend love and compassion to strangers. I smiled at the harried mom of two (one of them a *screaming* toddler) when others were rolling their eyes and muttering. I listened to the announcements and relayed them to an elderly woman with hearing aids. Then I listened to her as she told me about her children and grandchildren. I got to hear the story of a man who had never ventured far from home and who told me out of the blue, "It's good to be going home." Then he shared his wide-eyed account of a simple but once-in-a-lifetime trip to celebrate his fiftieth birthday. I made myself available to help a young couple, both blind, navigate the train. My trip became an adventure in responding to the Holy Spirit. I was a woman on a mundane but delightful mission I would have missed if I had been busy worrying.

7. Worship God. Raise your hands. Fall to your knees. Sing a song. Recite the ways God has cared for you and other people whose stories you know. There's no more effective way to take your eyes off yourself, connect with God and his perspective, and remind yourself what is true.

As we begin to apply this new perspective, let's explore a transformative view of one of the things we find most difficult to trust God with: the future.

7

The Future Belongs to God

In the recurring worries that consume so much of our emotional and mental energy, perhaps the most common element is their focus on an unknown future. We worry about what might happen, what seems likely, what is unlikely and even what's nearly impossible. Consider how many of your own worried thoughts begin with the words "What if . . . ?" When you stop to think about it, you may realize you have at least an occasional obsession with the uncertainty and inherent possibilities in what hasn't happened yet.

When I asked several people what they worry about, I heard a lot about the future. Cory told me he worries about what's going to happen at work, upcoming difficult conversations or other approaching situations. He mentioned he has learned to be more flexible and balanced than in the past, when he "focused more on controlling my future than trusting God." Cheryl, who calls herself "a planner," said, "I like to know what's coming, so if I don't I try to figure out how it can all work out. I've learned that's because I want security, and I try to make it for myself by knowing everything will work out." Deb worries about how her current job will affect her future career. And "sometimes I worry about knowing and hearing God's will for my life. When I don't get an answer to prayer, what does that mean? Which direction do I go?" And nearly everyone I talked to mentioned worry over their future finances.

We can all relate to these very common worries. The future is a source of anxiety, a world of possibility, and a place we cannot access. Yet so much of our worry is caused by our efforts to live there. While we should care about the future and recognize how today's choices shape tomorrow's consequences, it doesn't make sense for us to spend time worrying over what hasn't happened. Let's consider why.

What Is the Future?

So exactly what is the future? Merriam-Webster defines the future in three ways:

1. that is to be

2. of, relating to, or constituting a verb tense expressive of time yet to come

3. existing or occurring at a later time

By definition, the future doesn't exist. It "is to be," but it never *is*. We can't see, taste, touch, smell or hear it, so how do we recognize it? It's always beyond us, so does it ever arrive? Is it even real?

The future is a product of time, and physicists, who think professionally about such questions, generally agree that time does exist. But no physicist can explain and demonstrate exactly why it exists or how. And so far, physics has not been able to clearly demonstrate whether the future and the past simply are alive in our memories and our sense of anticipation or whether they continue to exist in parallel versions of our universe or alternate dimensions. Freaky, huh?

While we can't explain time without referring to time itself, it provides definition and boundary for our lives. We're aware of it nonstop, even when we don't think about it, and we may consider it a friend or our worst enemy—but we can't truly embrace or fight it. We know that it keeps moving at an objective level, regardless of whether we want it to or whether we're aware of it (for example, time does not stop while we're asleep). It exists outside our personal consciousness, and even if we throw away all our clocks, we can't choose to reject it or opt out, living apart from its effects.

In our universe, we measure time by its passing, and we measure its passing with spatial dimensions—with motion. Since ancient times, people have marked time by the sun's journey across the sky (actually, the rotation of the earth), sand falling through an hourglass, the changing patterns of stars in the night sky. Today we measure it with ticking hands around a clock face, a swinging pendulum, the regular pattern of changing digital numbers.

But if we did not measure time, we would still see the effects of its passing. Every day, we see beginnings and ends—both temporal concepts. Babies develop, enter our world and grow. Buildings crumble. Food spoils. Natural elements decay. The aging process for all living things shows in physical evidence long before it ends in death. For some reason, which we don't now understand, time moves forward. Unlike other physical laws and dimensions, time comes with a large-scale sense of constant progression and change.

That mysterious sense of forward motion is what defines and produces our inborn sense that the future exists. Where does the concept of the future come from? It's from our own awareness of the passage of time. The time we can discern is only the present—and the present is merely a flashing moment. But at some point early in our development, we experience enough of these fleeting moments that we become aware of a body of time we call the past and another body that someday will be, however briefly, a brand-new present.

Our awareness of relationship between the future, the past and the constantly flowing present can and should affect our behavior. The experience of consequences makes us aware that what we do now will profoundly influence what we will face in the future. But for all our understanding of cause and effect, we can't accurately predict the future. The world's most knowledgeable physicists could never account for the vast number of possibilities in any future event. Even the path of a smooth stone tumbling down a grassy hill is affected by countless variables. When human choices enter the picture, the idea of accurate prediction is laughable. Even the most impressive possible set of knowledge about the physical world and its laws, combined with a deep and insightful understanding of human behavior, can't tell us what will happen or help us control outcomes.

Whether it exists now in some other dimension or simply as a concept we understand because of our experience with the past, it is not within our power to place ourselves in the future. It is mysterious, but clearly an element without which our universe would not function as it does.

Essentially, for us the future is potential reality. It's unborn time, a powerful specter of possibility. We sense that it exists—and I believe it does exist in the world God inhabits—but we can't discern it, find it or own it.

THE FUTURE IS NOT OURS

When we worry, we fight the constraints of the way we and our world were created. We try to enter a place we can't go. We try to control what we have no power over. It's pointless. And it usually proves unwarranted.

How many times have you sat on an airplane either worrying or looking at the nervous faces of other passengers worrying their way through a flight? Chances are your flight didn't end in a crash. And when the plane pulled up to the gate, it turned out all that worry was a waste of time, energy and emotion.

I don't worry much about plane crashes, but I do have trouble sleeping the night before I travel, especially by air. It's not potential crashes that haunt me, but the series of circumstances involved in getting where I plan to go. The details I need to remember. The junction points where everything can go wrong. What if I forget to pack my toothbrush in the morning? What if my alarm clock doesn't go off? My car won't start or the taxi doesn't arrive on time? Traffic is locked in impassable clots? What if the offsite parking shuttle is too full and I have to wait for the next one and it doesn't get me to the airport on time? The check-in or security line is long, my gate is at the farthest possible point, and on the way to it I get stuck behind a slow-moving group of people who won't let me pass? Then when I get there, I find out my flight is cancelled? And even if I make my flight, what if I miss my connection? What if I forgot to pack something important? And did I accidentally pack a five-ounce bottle of flammable liquid?

For all my worry, I've never missed a flight (although I've had a few close calls). I've had some bad days, with cancelled flights and missed connections and yes, forgetting to pack something important. But even when things have gone wrong, I've survived these experiences and the sun has come up the next morning. My worry has never helped me, and the lost sleep was never worthwhile. I hate to think about all the breath I have spent on asking "What if . . . ?"

When the friend I mentioned in chapter six was expecting her first child and prenatal tests showed the potential of severe brain problems, she and her husband agonized over the possibilities and tried to prepare for an unknown future as parents. When their son was born healthy, it was obvious their worries had been for nothing.

But were their worries unproductive just because their son was born without severe health problems? If what they'd feared had happened, would their worries have accomplished anything? Yes, they still would have faced a serious challenge—perhaps the hardest thing they ever had faced. Their practical preparations would have helped them, as would their beginning the process of grief. But their worry would have done nothing more than burn much-needed emotional fuel.

Sometimes what illuminates worry's impotence is actually experiencing some of what we worry about. My friend and her husband were forced to trust God—but the right solution was not to trust him to make their baby healthy, to make them happy or to make their lives easy. They had to trust that whatever happened, God's sovereignty would not be thwarted. That his love, plans and purposes for them, and their child, would not be interrupted. That their grief would not overwhelm God; his redemptive work in them would continue and they could endure—and even thrive—through God's mysterious and limitless provision. That's not the same as trusting in religious-sounding clichés like "Everything happens for a reason" and "It will all work out in the end." When life gets hard, that's good reason for more trust in God, not less.

Another friend had a similar experience when she and her husband lost all their financial security. Both were self-employed in separate businesses, and when the Great Recession hit, both of their client lists dwindled. They had saved, invested and planned, but none of that mattered as they spent every dollar just to survive. They lost their house, sold their cars and many of their possessions, and started over. Now, a few years later, she says, "Funny thing is that during that couple-year spell, I actually found more joy and contentment as we simplified. We didn't have anything left to fall back on and had no idea where life was going next, but we seemed to savor moments and people that much more. We truly were living one day at a time." When a common worry—financial ruin—actually happened, they found they could survive without much of what they had been afraid to lose, and they even discovered new joy.

So what makes time move forward and bring the future into being? God does. He created time, still owns it, wrote the laws that regulate its power over us and lives in mastery over it. When we're trying to live in the future, we're trying to do something impossible. We're also wasting what God has given us for today on what he hasn't given us and may not give us.

We have no claim on the future; we're never there. God calls us to live in the present and gives us what we need to live in his strength, for "today's trouble is enough for today" (Mt 6:34). Worrying about the future means we at least partially ignore the gift of today and the calling we have to be in the place we are, with the people around us, in the circumstances we face in service to God. We make ourselves miserable, then reinforce our misery by inventing new possibilities. Sometimes we try to discern what will happen tomorrow, to prepare for every possibility and even to thwart the inevitable. Essentially, we try to be like God, who is not bound by the constraints of time, as the earth's original inhabitants tried to do when they kissed a beautiful temptation and found it tasted like bitter poison.

When we worry about the future, we usually imagine a world where God is nearly or completely absent, exaggerated in its sense of darkness, where bad things are almost sure to happen. We discount the active presence of God in this world, stemming the tide of darkness and self-destruction we seem so eager to throw ourselves into and acting for our benefit. We forget that with a loving and all-powerful God enacting his redemptive plan, the odds of something good happening are always at least as great as the odds of tragedy.

LIVING ON BORROWED TIME

What has God told us about our relationship with the future? How does he want us to view the coming days? Let's consider what Scripture says.

When God presented his laws for the people of Israel, he made clear that he hates occultic attempts to see into the future: "I will also turn against those who commit spiritual prostitution by putting their trust in mediums or in those who consult the spirits of the dead. I will cut them off from the community" (Lev 20:6).

This warning was repeated, in greater detail, to the next generation in Deuteronomy 18:10-12: "Do not let your people practice fortune-telling, or use sorcery, or interpret omens, or engage in witchcraft, or cast spells, or function as mediums or psychics, or call forth the spirits of the dead. Anyone who does these things is detestable to the Lord."

Generations later, the prophet Isaiah delivered another warning about such activities and one reason God finds them offensive: "Someone may say to you, 'Let's ask the mediums and those who consult the spirits of the dead. With their whisperings and mutterings, they will tell us what to do.' But shouldn't people ask God for guidance? Should the living seek guidance from the dead?" (Is 8:19).

Fortunetelling and similar activities are the opposite of seeking God; they attempt to circumvent the limits he has placed on our perception. The future belongs to God, and when we seek guidance from people who claim to see it, we reject what he offers us and the faith he asks of us. We try to reach outside our own realm—the present he has given us—and the resources he gives us when we depend on him for what we need.

God not only knows the future in general; he knows the personal future for each of us—and has since before we were born. In one of his most famous psalms, David wrote, "You saw me before I was born. Every day of my life was recorded in your book. Every moment was laid out before a single day had passed" (Ps 139:16). God wants us, like David, to trust in this truth: The future is not a mystery to God.

Although we can't see the future, we usually make plans based on our own assumptions about what will happen. But Proverbs 16:9 tells us we are always under God's sovereignty: "We can make our plans, but the LORD determines our steps." Isaiah 40 lends perspective to God's power over human plans—even plans made by the most powerful among us:

> God sits above the circle of the earth.
> The people below seem like grasshoppers to him!
> He spreads out the heavens like a curtain
> and makes his tent from them.

He judges the great people of the world
    and brings them all to nothing.
They hardly get started, barely taking root,
    when he blows on them and they wither.
    The wind carries them off like chaff. (vv. 22-24)

Ecclesiastes refers to both God's sovereignty and the futility of
making plans that assume life will carry on as it has in the past:

Accept the way God does things,
    for who can straighten what he has made crooked?
Enjoy prosperity while you can,
    but when hard times strike,
realize that both come from God.
    Remember that nothing is certain in this life.
        (Eccles 7:13-14)

Jesus also warned against planning and living as many of us do—as
if we will be here forever. He told a story, recorded in Luke 12:16-21,
of a rich man who owned a highly productive farm and had more
crops than he could use. So he decided to tear down his barns and
build bigger ones, then relax and live for years in the security of his
surplus. He failed to give proper attention to his relationship with
God, making plans as if he would always prosper and had plenty of
time to enjoy his wealth. But God called him a fool and told him
something he could not have known: "You will die this very night."

Similarly, James warned against making plans that ignore God's
authority over our lives, elevate our plans over his and assume we have
control over the future:

Look here, you who say, "Today or tomorrow we are going to a
certain town and will stay there a year. We will do business
there and make a profit." How do you know what your life will
be like tomorrow? Your life is like the morning fog—it's here a

little while, then it's gone. What you ought to say is, "If the Lord wants us to, we will live and do this or that." Otherwise you are boasting about your own plans, and all such boasting is evil. (Jas 4:13-16)

But the future is not only a place of forbidden mystery, a gift we may never receive. It is a reason for great hope for those who place their trust in Christ. Ultimately, our orientation toward the future should be as people whose own future doesn't end on this planet. Our lives are in God's hands, not only now but for eternity. As Paul told the Philippian church, "But we are citizens of heaven, where the Lord Jesus Christ lives. And we are eagerly waiting for him to return as our Savior. He will take our weak mortal bodies and change them into glorious bodies like his own, using the same power with which he will bring everything under his control" (Phil 3:20-21).

In his second letter to the Corinthian church, Paul wrote more about this hope and gave us a great example for how we should look at the future: "For our present troubles are small and won't last very long. Yet they produce for us a glory that vastly outweighs them and will last forever! So we don't look at the troubles we can see now; rather, we fix our gaze on things that cannot be seen. For the things we see now will soon be gone, but the things we cannot see will last forever" (2 Cor 4:17-18).

No book of the Bible speaks more about the future than the book of Revelation. Although many have claimed to understand its message in detail, no one can know for sure what future events it describes. Like all prophecies, its truths will be recognized when they unfold. But a few messages are clear. Among them, God knows the future, lives there and will not relinquish control of this world he created. "'I am the Alpha and the Omega—the beginning and the end,' says the Lord God. 'I am the one who is, who always was, and who is still to come—the Almighty One'" (Rev 1:8). Notice God proclaims he *is*, not *was,* the beginning. Although our world's creation is long past, he has not ceased to be the source of all things. He defines the beginning of time. Likewise, he will define the end of time as we know it. He is the one "who is still to come." He does not simply exist, enduring forever. Instead, our God is a very active presence in the future—acting and revealing himself in new ways as time unfolds for us.

Unknown but Certain

Francois de Fenelon, a great Christian leader in seventeenth-century France, wrote in a letter to an unknown recipient, "The future is not yet yours; it may never be. Live in the present moment. Tomorrow's grace is not given to you today. The present moment is the only place where you can touch the eternal realm."[1]

Ask yourself whether you're living in the future or trying to get there early. What does God want you to do in the present? When we worry about the future, we fail to truly trust God, to realize that he is already there. To God there is no future, no time, no constraints. He is not limited in the ways we are limited, and he can see everything we can't.

Does this mean we shouldn't plan for the future, dream about what is to come or prepare for possibilities? Of course not—worry is not the same as planning or preparation. Unlike making reasonable plans and preparations, trying to control the future or worrying over possibilities is completely unproductive. It accomplishes nothing, and it tries to take what only God has in exchange for what he has given us: the here and now.

When you think about the future, refuse to picture a future without God's love, grace and care for you and the people you love. The future may not look the way you want it to, but you will not be on your own. We all fear the unknown—but is there really any such thing in a world ruled by an omniscient God who has graciously and shockingly promised he will never abandon us? God is already there, and nothing surprises him. Nothing is unknown. As I tell my daughter when she worries about the approach of high school, "When you get there, you'll be ready." The key is to do what is before you today so you'll be ready for the future when it becomes the present.

When the future comes to haunt you, prayer is always a right response. But how should we pray in a way that combats worry? Try praying for God's will. When you don't know what else to say, breathe the prayer "Thy will be done." Thank God for living in the future and walking through it with you.

When you do have something specific to say, say it! Don't try to hide your worry from God. He is completely aware of what is happening in your mind, and he is able to interpret it much more clearly than you can. Remember, Jesus serves as our High Priest, an intermediary who goes before God on our behalf. "This High Priest of ours understands our weaknesses, for he faced all of the same testings we do, yet he did not sin" (Heb 4:15). In Jesus' life as a man living on earth, he had an awful lot he could have worried about. He understands exactly why you feel overwhelmed by your circumstances, your responsibilities and your uncertainty about the future. Lay it all out for him. As in any relationship, your honesty will build intimacy.

Then thank God that he is in control of all that worries you, that he lives in the future and will be there when you get there, that nothing mystifies him. Be quiet and allow the Holy Spirit to remind you of what the Bible teaches us about God's character and capabilities. Reminisce about the specific ways God has taken care of you and other people whose stories you know. Express your confidence in God's wisdom and love, even when life is a bruised and bloody mess. Acknowledge that God is not merely a nurse, a butler or a genie. He does not live to implement our plans or fulfill our dreams. He calls us to a life that finds meaning and joy in his plans, which produce much greater results than simply our own comfort and happiness. Reaffirm your commitment to trust him and to reject worry, and ask for his help in living up to that commitment. Then accept his peace and focus on what the next moment requires of you.

Living in God's peace does not mean denying reality. Faith and trust in God can give us the courage to face reality with greater boldness than we could muster on our own. As with Job, your worst fears may become reality: "What I always feared has happened to me. What I dreaded has come true" (Job 3:25). But as with him, God will give you strength and grace to declare in faith, "But as for me, I know that my Redeemer lives, and he will stand upon the earth at last" (Job 19:25). When the future seems threatening, imagine the worst and make peace with it as a possibility—but at the same time, recognize that it's probably unlikely. Also recognize that your worrying can't prevent it. Then look at it in light of God's truth and promises. Even if the worst happens, he'll be with you and will grant you a kind of strength you won't know until you need it.

At the same time, balance your perspective by imagining the best. Instead of worrying about the future, picture the marvelous possibilities—good things God might do in the future.

Keep in mind that while your future in this life is unknown, for every follower of Christ, the long-term future is certain and eternal. Take a lesson from the apostle Paul and refocus your gaze on what lies at the end of this dark and echoing tunnel, where you can see only the ground you stand on:

> For our present troubles are small and won't last very long. Yet they produce for us a glory that vastly outweighs them and will last forever! So we don't look at the troubles we can see now; rather, we fix our gaze on things that cannot be seen. For the things we see now will soon be gone, but the things we cannot see will last forever. (2 Cor 4:17-18)

The Bible—like common sense—makes clear that the future is not our domain. We have no claim on it, right to it, knowledge of it or assurance that it will ever arrive. The future belongs only to God, who rules and lives outside the limitations of time. And that same God is so good and beautiful, he has greater gifts in store for us than we can even imagine. Our unknowable future is bright!

8

The Fallacy of Possession

If the unknowable future is our most frequent cause for worry, perhaps our most gripping and powerful worries grow in the fertile soil of fears for the people and things we love—and we mistakenly believe belong to us.

Although we rarely discuss them in the same sermon or Bible study, it's no accident that right before Jesus' admonition to "consider the lilies of the field" in Matthew 6, he told his followers, "Don't store up treasures here on earth" (v. 19). When he said, "That is why I tell you not to worry about everyday life," he was referring to his previous sentence: "You cannot serve both God and money." He knew that our attachment to the treasures of this life was a primary cause for worry—and distraction from trusting and serving God.

Most of us are so busy storing up our treasures—in the form of the possessions and people we love—that we lose sight of the truth that everything and everyone belongs to God. He is the true owner of everything we think is ours and the one ultimately responsible for the people in our lives. He has granted us responsibility as stewards of riches and relationships, but he has not given us the ultimate responsibility that belongs only to him. We can experience freedom in recognizing our true role as caretakers, not owners.

We worry a lot about our possessions. And as people with plenty, we have much to worry about. I live in an area that is prone to flooding—not the old-fashioned kind that involves living on a flood plain, but the kind that happens when heavy rains overwhelm the storm sewer and the dirty water that's supposed to be flowing away from our neighborhood's houses instead backs up into them. As in other places, the weather in our area has grown more extreme in recent years, and in the seven years we have spent in our current home, we have been threatened with this kind of flooding at least two or three times each year. Thanks be to God, a former owner installed a backflow valve in the house—we discovered this by accident after we moved in. If we hadn't closed this valve each time water threatened, we would have had serious (and disgusting) flooding.

But just because it hasn't happened yet doesn't mean it won't happen. What if one of these torrential rainstorms happens while we're away from home and we can't get back in time to manually close the valve? Our carpet, drywall and electronics would be ruined, along with furniture and possibly appliances like our washer and dryer and our hot water heater.

Several of our friends and neighbors have had significant flooding in their basements in recent years. So nowadays, when I see a big rainstorm coming, my stomach threatens to turn inside out. I worry about our house and our belongings. Usually, I also recognize the irony in this worry. If I didn't have so much—a nice, comfortable house with a basement, carpet, computers and upholstered furniture, I'd have far less anxiety about flooding because I would have much less at stake.

We all worry about the risks that come with modern abundance: cars break down, investments lose money, appliances stop working, refrigerators and freezers aren't any good when the power goes out.

We feel we need most of these conveniences, and we think we own them. Although we aren't wrong to have washers and dryers, carpet and vacuum cleaners, we are wrong to believe they are ours or that God has given them to us merely for our own comfort and happiness. If we held them loosely, we'd have far less to worry about.

Our treasures aren't just material goods. We are tremendously possessive of people as well, and the misconception that they are ours generates a lot of worry—particularly for parents.

Treasured People

When I asked several people why they worry, one friend answered, "I worry because I love." She also told me, "Being a mom inherently means worry. All the dangers lurking out there in the world can really paralyze me when it comes to my kids." Whether parents or not, we can all relate to that statement. We worry about people we love.

As I mentioned earlier, my mother has schizophrenia. Schizophrenia is a cyclical disorder, and most people who have it go through times of relative stability and times of great instability. Unfortunately, unstable periods can have dramatic consequences—people wander off, commit crimes, find themselves homeless with no idea who they are or where they came from, become victims of violence, live in terror of the dangers their delusions and paranoia tell them are very real and imminent. Although my mom takes medication and receives psychiatric care, her illness makes her vulnerable, and she has cycled through these times of instability since I was fourteen years old.

When Mom is going through a period of instability, my family tries our best to take good care of her, but sometimes we are forced to recognize that she has wandered outside the scope of our care. When she left home without leaving much of a trace, we tried to track her down and laid awake at night, visualizing bad things that could happen to her. When she rejected her faith in Christ and dove into the occult, we grieved and worried over her spiritual condition. After she was convicted of a crime while living in a homeless shelter and not taking medication, we agonized when she went to prison, imagining mistreatment and despair. But ultimately, for all our worry, we couldn't control what happened in those situations.

As I lay in bed one night, grieving over Mom's troubles, begging God to help her and asking him to show me what to do, I heard God speak to me and assure me that Mom was not outside his care. He had not and would not let go of her—but I had to let go. I had to acknowledge that Mom was in God's hands, physically and spiritually. I had to admit that terrible things could happen to her (and some did), but I couldn't prevent them, and my worry was worthless. My prayers and my love were the very best ministry I could offer both her and me.

As my friend pointed out, parents are especially prone to worry—worry comes as a side dish with the tremendous helping of responsibility in raising children. Another friend told me, "I also worry about my children in this ever-changing world—will they be passionate followers of Christ and will they be able to hold strong with everything else beating loudly for their love and attention?"

The first night after my husband and I brought our oldest daughter home from the hospital, I crept over to her crib multiple times to make sure she was still breathing. Now she's a teenager, and I'll confess I still can't go to sleep until I make sure she and her younger sister are breathing.

Race to Nowhere is a 2009 documentary that highlights one cancerous effect of parental worry, specifically about their kids' chances at success in life. "Featuring the heartbreaking stories of students across the country who have been pushed to the brink by over-scheduling, over-testing and the relentless pressure to achieve," this film offers compelling evidence of how performance pressure is hurting children. As parents feel pressure from an educational and cultural system that preys on their fears, they push kids to perform to some undefined optimal standard.

Kids respond, often with hard work and high achievement, but they also pay with high levels of anxiety, display psychological and physical illnesses, resort to habitual cheating, sometimes burn out before they're twenty, and struggle to discover who they are and what they want to do. The irony is that all this pressure, anxiety and high performance are pointless. They don't produce happier, smarter or more fulfilled children or adults; they just produce anxious people who know how to work the system (in the film, one teacher calls them "robots") but never reach that elusive goal called success.[1]

All people belong to God, not to us. Parents, our kids don't belong to us. God has called us to positions of responsibility in our children's lives. But we do not have ultimate responsibility for them—God does. It does no good—in fact, it causes harm—for us to worry over them and try to adopt a measure of control we do not have. We need to entrust them to God.

This is true not only for parents. Many of us worry about friends and relatives, as I do about my mom. Some worry about people they don't know, like those who don't follow Christ or who live in poverty or suffer under persecution. We are right to care about all such people. We are right to care *for* them as we can and as our care will help, not hurt. But we aren't right to try to control them, to take ownership of their spiritual destiny, to push them into the life we want for them. They all belong to God, who has called us to love and to pray, and to take action as God's Spirit calls and equips us to do so. But he never calls us to worry.

IT ALL BELONGS TO GOD

Given that God has created our universe and rules over all, it makes sense that he owns everything and everyone. But does he exert this sense of ownership at the individual level? Does he really want us to relinquish our illusion of control and defer to his responsibility of ownership for individual people and things? Let's look at what several Bible passages say on that question.

When God presents his laws to the people of Israel, he includes rules for distribution and ownership of property. For one thing, each family would be granted its allotment of land, which could not be permanently sold to someone else. God's justification for establishing such rules is in his declaration that ultimately the land belongs to him: "The land must never be sold on a permanent basis, for the land belongs to me. You are only foreigners and tenant farmers working for me" (Lev 25:23).

When Moses speaks to a new generation of the people of Israel, after their parents have died and before they take possession of the Promised Land, he presents them with the Ten Commandments God had written on stone tablets forty years before. As he introduces these commands, he reminds them of God's authority to present such rules: "Look, the highest heavens and the earth and everything in it all belong to the LORD your God" (Deut 10:14).

Generations later, when King David commissions the building of the temple his son Solomon will oversee, he acknowledges God's ownership of everything he, as king, could have claimed as his own: "Yours, O LORD, is the greatness, the power, the glory, the victory, and the majesty. Everything in the heavens and on earth is yours, O LORD, and this is your kingdom. We adore you as the one who is over all things." He even recognizes God's ownership of what the people have collected to be used in building: "O LORD our God, even this material we have gathered to build a Temple to honor your holy name comes from you! It all belongs to you!" (1 Chron 29:11, 16).

David writes on this theme in Psalm 24 as well:

The earth is the LORD's, and everything in it.
    The world and all its people belong to him.
For he laid the earth's foundation on the seas
    and built it on the ocean depths. (vv. 1-2)

In well-known lyrics repurposed in a twentieth-century hymn,

Psalm 50 also emphasizes the truth that God owns everything and needs nothing from us:

> For all the animals of the forest are mine,
>> and I own the cattle on a thousand hills.
> I know every bird on the mountains,
>> and all the animals of the field are mine.
> If I were hungry, I would not tell you,
>> for all the world is mine and everything in it. (vv. 10-12)

In a reassuring and inspired proclamation of his power, God spoke through the prophet Isaiah. His words assure us that he speaks and calls directly to each new generation. Regardless of how little faith we may have in the generations that follow us, God's work in people will not die with us: "Who has done such mighty deeds, summoning each new generation from the beginning of time? It is I, the LORD, the First and the Last. I alone am he" (Is 41:4).

Nebuchadnezzar, king of ancient Babylon, learned a hard lesson about God's sovereignty. As he brags about his own power and the kingdom he rules, he hears from God with a severe correction. God speaks to him and tells him his kingdom will be taken from him immediately and he will live as an outcast, like a wild animal. This will last "until you learn that the Most High rules over the kingdoms of the world and gives them to anyone he chooses." After a time, Nebuchadnezzar looks toward heaven and his sanity returns. He praises God and acknowledges him as the true ruler of everything: "His rule is everlasting, and his kingdom is eternal. All the people of the earth are nothing compared to him" (Dan 4:32, 34-35).

Through the prophet Haggai, God assures his people that the ruined temple will be rebuilt—a task that seems impossible. But it is far from impossible with God: "The silver is mine, and the gold is mine, says the LORD of Heaven's Armies" (Hag 2:8).

Later, Jesus himself says some shocking words in making the point that we are not to cling tightly to our relationships with others (or even our own lives), even in our own families. Our love and commitment to Christ must dwarf our love for anyone else: "If you want to be my disciple, you must hate everyone else by comparison—your father and mother, wife and children, brothers and sisters—yes, even your own life. Otherwise, you cannot be my disciple" (Lk 14:26).

In a letter to Christians in Corinth, the apostle Paul establishes that even Christians' faith and discernment do not belong to us: "What do you have that God hasn't given you? And if everything you have is from God, why boast as though it were not a gift?" (1 Cor 4:7). Paul also points out that even our bodies are not our own: "Don't you realize that your body is the temple of the Holy Spirit, who lives in you and was given to you by God? You do not belong to yourself, for God bought you with a high price. So you must honor God with your body" (1 Cor 6:19-20).

And in his letter to the Colossian church, Paul reminds us all that Christ is responsible for our very existence—and the existence of everything we can and cannot see, even the things we fear:

> Christ is the visible image of the invisible God.
>> He existed before anything was created and is supreme over
>> all creation,
> for through him God created everything
>> in the heavenly realms and on earth.
> He made the things we can see
>> and the things we can't see—
> such as thrones, kingdoms, rulers, and authorities in the
>> unseen world.
>> Everything was created through him and for him. (Col 1:15-16)

Finally, the apostle Peter writes about our spiritual gifts, which also don't belong to us. They come from God, not simply for our own enjoyment but to serve one another and so that "everything you do will bring glory to God through Jesus Christ. All glory and power to him forever and ever! Amen" (1 Pet 4:11).

Our sense of possession is a fallacy. Our desire to cling to what we don't own is foolish and enslaves us to fear. It elevates our sense of self-importance and keeps us from living in boldness and freedom to respond to God's Holy Spirit. Everything and everyone we care about belongs to God. He has entrusted us with material goods, spiritual gifts, talents and abilities, relationships, opportunities and experiences so we will take good care of them, encourage their potential, grow in faith and faithfulness, worship God with what he has given us and ultimately bring him greater glory on earth. And yes, in the process experience deep joy. But we do not have ownership—and this is a good thing. The people and things that mean so much to us are all better off in God's hands than ours. If we can live as if this is true, we'll have a lot less to worry about.

LETTING GO

It's easy, and discouraging, to think that if we're not supposed to worry, we'll have to stop caring about what worries us. But rejecting worry does not mean apathy. Living worry-free means we actually have more energy to truly care about and for the issues and people who are important to us. We shouldn't address worry by trying to diminish our care for what matters—but rather than waste energy on worry, we can respond to God with trust and with action as appropriate. We can focus on what God calls us to do, work less, spend more time with family, laugh more, get better sleep, play more, pray more, serve more, eat well, follow the direction of the Holy Spirit and stop doing things that are motivated by worry. We can stop working against God's work in other people—and in ourselves. We can live life to the full (Jn 10:10), as God has called us to do, in the present.

To give up your inappropriate grasp on what belongs to God, really spend time in this chapter. Do you believe that everything and everyone belongs to God? Wrestle over what that means. Are you holding on to what you shouldn't?

Let go of your possessive grip on people and things. Let go of your desire to control what is not yours. Try making a list of people and things you feel responsible for. Ask God to give you wisdom to see your true role in relationship to them. Write down what God has actually asked of you. For example, for your children you might list "Teach them about Christ" and "Help them discover who God made them to be." For your spouse you might write, "Be a faithful friend and partner" and "Always be truthful and trustworthy." For your home you might write, "Welcome friends and strangers."

When your list is complete, spend some time considering what needs to change in your life to bring yourself into proper relationship with people and possessions. Do you need to stop trying to manipulate someone into making the choices you think are right for them? Invite someone into your home when you'd rather keep it clean and quiet or you're feeling insecure because it's not perfect? Make peace with the possibility that someone you love will meet with tragedy?

You don't truly own anything, and while you're responsible for the way you treat others, you are not ultimately responsible for anyone else's choices. Reject guilt based in a false sense of responsibility.

May we learn to authentically echo what God's ancient people affirmed:

I came naked from my mother's womb,
  and I will be naked when I leave.
The LORD gave me what I had,
  and the LORD has taken it away.
Praise the name of the LORD! (Job 1:21)

Even though the fig trees have no blossoms
  and there are no grapes on the vines;
even though the olive crop fails,

and the fields lie empty and barren;
even though the flocks die in the fields,
and the cattle barns are empty,
yet I will rejoice in the LORD!
I will be joyful in the God of my salvation!
The Sovereign LORD is my strength!
He makes me as surefooted as a deer,
able to tread upon the heights. (Hab 3:17-19)

How I praise the Lord that you are concerned about me again. I know you have always been concerned for me, but you didn't have the chance to help me. Not that I was ever in need, for I have learned how to be content with whatever I have. I know how to live on almost nothing or with everything. I have learned the secret of living in every situation, whether it is with a full stomach or empty, with plenty or little. For I can do everything through Christ, who gives me strength. (Phil 4:10-13)

9

Who Do You Trust?

Less than two hours from our home in the suburbs of Chicago is Starved Rock State Park, with a landscape very different from what most would expect to find in the middle of Illinois. Its cliffs, canyons, waterfalls and trails make it a great place for a hike, and we usually spend a day there at least once a year.

A year or two ago, we visited Starved Rock with some friends who, like us, had preteen girls. At one point, the girls enthusiastically climbed partway up a canyon wall for the same reason most people climb anything these days: it was there.

Once they decided they had gone far enough, they realized coming down was scarier than going up, and they nervously clung to the rock. Soon their dads made their way over to the canyon wall, stood at the bottom and encouraged the girls to come down. Suddenly more confident, the girls became sure-footed and quick and shortly found themselves back on the path at the bottom. The dads didn't catch any kids or even give anyone a hand to grasp. But their simple presence made all the difference. Although nothing about the climb had changed, the girls' trust in their dads made them stop worrying, helped them find confidence and courage and made the descent easier.

I close with another parenting-related metaphor, this one biblical:

LORD, my heart is not proud;
> my eyes are not haughty.
I don't concern myself with matters too great
> or too awesome for me to grasp.
Instead, I have calmed and quieted myself,
> like a weaned child who no longer cries for its mother's milk.
> Yes, like a weaned child is my soul within me.
O Israel, put your hope in the LORD—
> now and always. (Ps 131)

Although most (or maybe all) of us don't remember the experience of weaning from our mothers or moving from bottle feedings to mushy food served from tiny spoons, most moms will tell you the process is laced with at least some level of anxiety for everyone involved. It's a time of transition an infant can't possibly understand, even if her rapidly changing brain and digestive system are telling her she wants to eat what the grown-ups eat. It's a time for essential maturation, an opportunity to learn self-feeding and self-soothing skills she will need for the rest of her life. At the same time, her days of dependency aren't over; she still must rely on trusted adults to provide what she needs. And if she has been treated with love and kindness, those days of absolute dependency will be a foundation for the kind of trust so critical for a healthy childhood. That trust is one of the reasons a young child can calm and soothe herself in healthy ways—she knows someone else is still concerned "with matters too great or too awesome for [her] to grasp."

For mothers, this can be a time of anxiety (and perhaps relief) as well. Along with delight, the experience of seeing her child grow in independence and capability can produce grief and fear. No mom knows what lies ahead for her child. And every mom can be certain she will fail her child's trust on at least a few occasions.

In this way God is not like us. He knows all that is next, and his parenting skills are perfect. His vision and plans are grander than our own—even if they don't always satisfy our longing for comfort and ease in this life. If we can't trust the powerful, wise, generous and loving God of the universe, who can we trust? It certainly doesn't make sense to place our faith in fragile people like ourselves.

I hope that as we focus on who God is, and acknowledge who we are by comparison, you and I will develop childlike trust in our Heavenly Parent. I pray that our worries will wilt in his shadow and that we will grow in freedom and courage to live the bold kind of life he calls us to.

Why Trust God?

He never fails

He never leaves us

He never disappoints us

He loves us unconditionally

He's the creator of all things

He transforms us from the inside

He forgives our sins

He knows everything

He rules the future

He is all-powerful

He is everywhere

He is good

He is great

He Is

A Word About Anxiety Disorders

Anxiety disorders" is an umbrella term for a specific category of mental illness. Disorders of this type involve uncontrolled anxiety, which overwhelms those who suffer. While anxiety is not always healthy, a certain level is normal, even if that anxiety peaks during times of stress or immediate threat. For people with anxiety disorders, anxiety reaches a level that consistently interferes with daily functioning. And sometimes that interference may be severe and even debilitating.

People with anxiety disorders experience the same effects of anxiety that everyone else does: worry, stress, elevated heart rate, shortness of breath and sweating, among others. The difference is they may experience these effects to a greater degree than people without such disorders. Or they may experience them for long periods of time, after the threat has passed or for what seems like no reason at all. They also may experience some more disruptive symptoms of anxiety, such as obsessive thoughts, compulsive actions, flashbacks to traumatic events, extreme sleeplessness, intense and paralyzing fear, and an overall sense of dread.

People with anxiety disorders may experience panic attacks and an overwhelming urge to flee because their threat-response systems are stuck in fourth gear and their bodies believe they are in imminent danger. They may suddenly feel desperately ill in a stressful situation, unable to focus or interact with others. They may become obsessed with cleanliness and ritualistic behaviors. Some might be unable to mentally leave a traumatic situation, even if it happened decades in the past. Their suffering bodies and minds experience natural processes in unnatural ways. Because their minds and bodies believe trauma is at hand, they respond as they were designed to. The problem is, this response is unwanted and unnecessary. It's also life-altering.

For people with anxiety disorders, symptoms may or may not be tied to a certain trigger, such as worry over a specific situation. For some people, it may be triggered by an incident, such as a traumatic event, but then grow into a general sense of anxiety that is out of control. For others, an anxiety disorder begins as a generalized issue, not tied to any specific event or worry.

Anxiety disorders are some of the most common forms of mental illness in the United States. According to the National Institute of Mental Health, every year 18 percent of American adults experience some kind of anxiety disorder. Of these cases, 22 percent are considered severe.[1] Some specific anxiety disorders include agoraphobia, generalized anxiety disorder, obsessive-compulsive disorder (OCD), panic disorder, post-traumatic stress disorder, social anxiety disorder and specific phobias.

Because mental illness of all kinds is stigmatized in our culture, most people are not eager to share openly about such illnesses and disorders, including anxiety disorders. Such stigma discourages people from seeking treatment and getting help when they need it. Many Christians consider anxiety disorders, and other mental illness, signs of weakness or self-indulgence that should be condemned. However, this is no more true of anxiety disorders than it is of conditions we openly discuss without shame such as heart disease, cancer, diabetes, autoimmune disorders, allergies, arthritis and scoliosis. People whose natural anxious response malfunctions do not deserve our judgment. And as long as the rest of us do stand in judgment of them, blaming them for their illness and telling them to have more faith and pray more, many will not get the help they need.

Although many people who experience anxiety disorders and panic attacks feel a powerful sense of shame, I don't believe people with anxiety disorders should be condemned. (For a detailed view of my perspective on mental illness and its relationship to the church, see my book *Troubled Minds,* published by InterVarsity Press.) In fact, I find it ironic that any of the rest of us should judge them for their involuntary symptoms while failing to identify the voluntary habit of worry in our own lives.

If you suffer with an anxiety disorder, I desperately don't want you to feel condemned or shamed in this book. You don't need condemnation; you have a medical condition that needs treatment. You may not choose to worry any more than the rest of us; your mind and body simply respond more powerfully to anxiety than most people's do. Despite what some may suggest, your anxiety disorder is not your fault, and the answer is not as simple as "pray more" or "have more faith." You need help from a counselor, psychologist or psychiatrist who can help you identify the errors in your mind and body that are causing your symptoms. You may need to take medication for a short time or for many years, and you will need to correct your underlying thought patterns and emotional reactions.

This book ultimately points readers to trust in our God, who is stronger than we can imagine and more loving than we can understand. However, this book will not "cure" or treat a disorder. If you feel you may have symptoms of an anxiety disorder, please get help from a mental health professional who can help you find relief.

Inspiration for the Worried

This special section will give you an opportunity to focus on God, who sees all and knows all and never loses control of all that worries us. Let this inspiring truth remind you why trusting God is the only sensible way to live in a world we can't control and in the face of a future we can't see.

This is who our God is.

Have you never heard?
    Have you never understood?
The LORD is the everlasting God,
    the Creator of all the earth.
He never grows weak or weary.
    No one can measure the depths of his understanding.
He gives power to the weak
    and strength to the powerless.
Even youths will become weak and tired,
    and young men will fall in exhaustion.

But those who trust in the LORD will find new strength.
    They will soar high on wings like eagles.
They will run and not grow weary.
    They will walk and not faint. (Is 40:28-31)

≈

Where were you when I laid the foundations of the earth?
    Tell me, if you know so much.
Who determined its dimensions
    and stretched out the surveying line?
What supports its foundations,
    and who laid its cornerstone
as the morning stars sang together
    and all the angels shouted for joy? (Job 38:4-7)

≈

Look at the birds. They don't plant or harvest or store food in barns, for your heavenly Father feeds them. And aren't you far more valuable to him than they are? (Mt 6:26)

≈

The grass withers and the flowers fade
    beneath the breath of the LORD.
    And so it is with people.
The grass withers and the flowers fade,
    but the word of our God stands forever. (Is 40:7-8)

≈

At the moment I have all I need—and more! I am generously supplied with the gifts you sent me with Epaphroditus. They are a sweet-smelling sacrifice that is acceptable and pleasing to God. And this same God who takes care of me will supply all your needs from his glorious riches, which have been given to us in Christ Jesus. (Phil 4:18-19)

≈

You will keep in perfect peace
    all who trust in you,
    all whose thoughts are fixed on you!
Trust in the LORD always,
    for the LORD GOD is the eternal Rock.
He humbles the proud
    and brings down the arrogant city.
    He brings it down to the dust.
The poor and oppressed trample it underfoot,
    and the needy walk all over it. (Is 26:3-6)

≈

What is the price of two sparrows—one copper coin? But not a single sparrow can fall to the ground without your Father knowing it. And the very hairs on your head are all numbered. So don't be afraid; you are more valuable to God than a whole flock of sparrows. (Mt 10:29-31)

≈

Some nations boast of their chariots and horses,
    but we boast in the name of the LORD our God.
Those nations will fall down and collapse,
    but we will rise up and stand firm. (Ps 20:7-8)

≈

What shall we say about such wonderful things as these? If God is for us, who can ever be against us? (Rom 8:31)

≈

Let all that I am wait quietly before God,
    for my hope is in him.
He alone is my rock and my salvation,
    my fortress where I will not be shaken.
My victory and honor come from God alone.
    He is my refuge, a rock where no enemy can reach me.
O my people, trust in him at all times.
    Pour out your heart to him,
    for God is our refuge. (Ps 62:5-8)

≈

Then I saw a new heaven and a new earth, for the old heaven and the old earth had disappeared. And the sea was also gone. And I saw the holy city, the new Jerusalem, coming down from God out of heaven like a bride beautifully dressed for her husband.

I heard a loud shout from the throne, saying, "Look, God's home is now among his people! He will live with them, and they will be his people. God himself will be with them. He will wipe every tear from their eyes, and there will be no more death or sorrow or crying or pain. All these things are gone forever." (Rev 21:1-4)

Amen.

Notes

CHAPTER 1: FRANTIC

[1] World Health Organization, "Injuries and Violence: The Facts" (Geneva, Switzerland: World Health Organization, 2010), http://apps.who.int/iris/bitstream/10665/44288/1/9789241599375_eng.pdf.

[2] Centers for Disease Control and Prevention, *National Antimicrobial Resistance Monitoring System (NARMS)—Frequently Asked Questions (FAQ) About Antibiotic Resistance* (Atlanta: U.S. Department of Health and Human Services, Centers for Disease Control and Prevention, 2005), www.cdc.gov/narms/faq.html.

[3] Coco Ballantyne, "Strange but True: Antibacterial Products May Do More Harm Than Good," *Scientific American* (June 7, 2007), www.scientificamerican.com/article.cfm?id=strange-but-true-antibacterial-products-may-do-more-harm-than-good.

[4] Benjamin James Sadock and Virginia Alcott Sadock, *Kaplan & Sadock's Concise Textbook of Clinical Psychiatry, Third Edition* (Philadelphia: Lippincott Williams & Wilkins, 2008), p. 236.

[5] Ibid.

[6] Edward H. Hallowell, "Fighting Life's 'What Ifs,'" *Psychology Today*, November 1, 1997, www.psychologytoday.com/articles/199711/fighting-lifes-what-ifs.

CHAPTER 2: OUR WORRIED WORLD

[1] JoHannah Reardon, "I Gave Up Worry for Lent," www.johannahreardon.com/2012/02/22/i-gave-up-worry-for-lent.

[2] Barry Glassner, *The Culture of Fear: Why Americans Are Afraid of the Wrong Things* (New York: Basic Books, 1999), p. xxviii.

[3] According to the US Department of Justice, there were an estimated 115 "stereotypical kidnappings" ("abductions perpetrated by a stranger or slight acquaintance and involving a child who was transported 50 or more miles, detained

overnight, held for ransom or with the intent to keep the child permanently, or killed") in 1999, the most recent year for which they have done detailed study. David Finkelhor, Heather Hammer and Andrea J. Sedlak, "Nonfamily Abducted Children: National Estimates and Characteristics," *NISMART* (Washington, DC: US Department of Justice, 2002), p. 2, www.ncjrs.gov /pdffiles1/ojjdp/196467.pdf.

[4]Lenore Skenazy, "Why I Let My 9-year-Old Ride the Subway Alone," *New York Sun,* April 1, 2008, www.nysun.com/opinion/why-i-let-my-9-year-old -ride-subway-alone/73976.

[5]William J. Bushaw and Shane J. Lopez, "A Time for Change: The 42nd Annual Phi Delta Kappa/Gallup Poll of the Public's Attitudes Toward the Public Schools," *Kappan Magazine,* September 2010.

[6]Maryn McKenna, "The Enemy Within: A New Pattern of Antibiotic Resistance," *Scientific American,* March 22, 2011, www.scientificamerican.com/article .cfm?id=the-enemy-within.

[7]Barry Schwartz, *The Paradox of Choice: Why More Is Less* (New York: Harper-Collins, 2004), p. 104.

Chapter 3: Worry's Many Destructive Powers

[1]Dr. Seuss, *How the Grinch Stole Christmas!* (New York: Random House, 1957).

[2]Jeff Nilsson, "The Predictor Who Got It Right (Mostly)," *The Saturday Evening Post,* December 31, 2011, www.saturdayeveningpost.com/2011/12/31/archives/ then-and-now/predictor.html.

[3]American Psychological Association, "Stress in America Findings" (Washington, DC: APA, November 9, 2010), p. 12, www.apa.org/news/press/releases/ stress/2010/national-report.pdf.

[4]Suzanne Pieper, Jos F. Brosschot, Rien van der Leeden and Julian F. Thayer, "Prolonged Cardiac Effects of Momentary Assessed Stressful Events and Worry Episodes," *Psychosomatic Medicine,* April 21, 2010, www.psychosomatic medicine.org/content/72/6/570.abstract.

[5]WebMD, "How Worrying Affects the Body," www.webmd.com/balance/how -worrying-affects-your-body.

[6]Ibid.

[7]Ibid.

[8]Edward H. Hallowell, "Fighting Life's 'What Ifs,'" *Psychology Today,* November 1, 1997, www.psychologytoday.com/articles/199711/fighting-lifes-what-ifs.

9 National Institute of Mental Health, "Statistics: Any Anxiety Disorder Among Adults," www.nimh.nih.gov/statistics/1ANYANX_ADULT.shtml.

10 National Institute of Mental Health, "Anxiety Disorders: Panic Disorder," www.nimh.nih.gov/health/publications/anxiety-disorders/panic-disorder .shtml.

11 American Psychological Association, *Stress in America: Our Health at Risk* (Washington, DC: American Psychological Association, 2012), www.apa.org/ news/press/releases/stress/2011/final-2011.pdf.

12 Camille Peri, "What Lack of Sleep Does to Your Mind," *WebMD*, www.webmd .com/sleep-disorders/excessive-sleepiness-10/emotions-cognitive.

13 D. J. Taylor, K. L. Lichstein, H. H. Durrence et al., "Epidemiology of insomnia, depression, and anxiety," *Sleep* 28, no. 11 (2005): 1457-64.

14 Karen Springen, "7 Myths About Sleep," *Marie Claire*, April 6, 2007, www .marieclaire.com/health-fitness/advice/myths-sleep.

15 National Sleep Foundation, "How Much Sleep Do We Really Need?" www .sleepfoundation.org/article/how-sleep-works/how-much-sleep-do-we-really -need.

16 Ibid.

17 National Sleep Foundation, "Annual Sleep in America Poll Exploring Connections with Communications Technology Use and Sleep," press release, March 7, 2011, www.sleepfoundation.org/article/press-release/annual-sleep-america -poll-exploring-connections-communications-technology-use-.

18 Anne Harding, "Alcohol and Anxiety a Risky Mix for Some," CNN.com, August 1, 2011, www.cnn.com/2011/HEALTH/08/01/alcohol.anxiety.risky .health/index.html.

19 Rick Nauert, "Excessive Worry Harms Interpersonal Relationships," *Psych-Central* (2011): http://psychcentral.com/news/2011/07/27/excessive-worry -harms-interpersonal-relationships/28081.html.

20 American Psychological Association, "Stress in America Findings," press release, November 9, 2010, p. 9, www.apa.org/news/press/releases/stress/2010 /national-report.pdf.

21 Sandra Block, "$2 Trillion Wiped out of Retirement Funds," *USA Today*, October 8, 2008, www.usatoday.com/money/perfi/retirement/2008-10-07 -retirement-accounts-losses_N.htm.

22 Governors Highway Safety Association, "Cell Phone and Texting Laws," May 2012, www.ghsa.org/html/stateinfo/laws/cellphone_laws.html.

23 National Highway Traffic Safety Administration, "What Is Distracted Driving?"

Distraction.gov, www.distraction.gov/content/get-the-facts/facts-and
-statistics.html.

[24] Harris Interactive, "Large Majority of Drivers Who Own Cell Phones Use
Them While Driving Even Though They Know This Is Dangerous," press release, June 8, 2009, www.nsc.org/safety_road/Distracted_Driving/Documents/
Large%20majority%20of%20drivers%20who%20own%20cell%20phones%20
use%20them.pdf.

[25] Cotton Delo, "Why Companies Are Cozying Up to Napping at Work," CNN
Money, August 18, 2011, http://management.fortune.cnn.com/2011/08/18/why
-companies-are-cozying-up-to-napping-at-work.

CHAPTER 4: WHAT GOD SAYS ABOUT WORRY

[1] *Strong's Exhaustive Concordance of the Bible*, s.v., "*'arats,*" www.biblestudytools
.com/concordances/strongs-exhaustive-concordance.

[2] Ibid., s.v., "*raphah.*"

[3] Ibid., s.v., "*charadah.*"

[4] Ibid., s.v., "*tarasso.*"

CHAPTER 6: IT'S ALL ABOUT PERSPECTIVE

[1] See National Association of Cognitive-Behavioral Therapists (NACBT), www
.nacbt.org/whatiscbt.htm.

[2] Andrew Newberg and Mark Robert Waldman, *How God Changes Your Brain*
(New York: Ballantine Books, 2009), p. 5.

[3] Ibid., p. 145.

[4] Ibid., p. 146.

[5] Timothy R. Jennings, *The God-Shaped Brain* (Downers Grove, IL: InterVarsity
Press, 2013), p. 47.

[6] Ibid, p. 56.

[7] Ibid.

[8] Tyler Wigg-Stevenson, *The World Is Not Ours to Save* (Downers Grove, IL:
InterVarsity Press, 2013), p. 55.

CHAPTER 7: THE FUTURE BELONGS TO GOD

[1] Francois de Fenelon, *The Seeking Heart* (Jacksonville, FL: SeedSowers, 1992),
p. 94.

Chapter 8: The Fallacy of Possession

[1]"About the Film," *Race to Nowhere,* dir. Vicki Abeles, www.racetonowhere.com/about-film.

Appendix A: A Word About Anxiety Disorders

[1]National Institute of Mental Health, "Statistics," www.nimh.nih.gov/statistics/index.shtml.

About the Author

Amy Simpson is an editor at Christianity Today, leading publishing efforts for GiftedforLeadership.com and serving as senior editor of *Leadership Journal*. Amy is a freelance writer, contributor to many church ministry resources and author of *Troubled Minds: Mental Illness and the Church's Mission* (InterVarsity Press). She also serves as a Co-Active coach and enjoys coming alongside people to help them own their purpose, step forward and live in truth.

Amy grew up a pastor's daughter, in the shadow of her mother's schizophrenia, and with an anxious drive to achieve peace and self-worth through her own efforts. Her personal experience in the trap of anxiety, and her ongoing journey to greater trust in God, qualify her to write on this topic with authority, empathy and inspiration.

Amy is married to Trevor Simpson, a licensed certified professional counselor, and is mom to two girls. They live in Illinois.

amysimpsononline.com
twitter.com/aresimpson

IVP *Crescendo*
COURAGE. CONFIDENCE. CALLING.

Some voices challenge us. Others support or encourage us. Voices can move us to change our minds, draw close to God, discover a new spiritual gift. The voices of others are shaping who we are.

The voices behind IVP Crescendo join together to draw us into God's story. We'll discover God's work around the globe even as we learn to love the people around the corner. We'll have opportunity to heal our places of pain. We'll discover new ways to love our families. We'll hear God's voice speaking into our lives as we discover new places of influence.

IVP Crescendo invites you to join in the rising chorus

- *to listen to the voices of others*
- *to hear the voice of God*
- *and to grow your own voice in*

COURAGE. CONFIDENCE. CALLING.

ivpress.com/crescendo
ivpress.com/crescendo-social